# FISHING AND HUNTING STORIES

## FROM
## THE LAKE OF THE WOODS

Dr. Duane R. Lund

Filled with scores of tips
for greater success.

*Distributed by*
Adventure Publications
P. O. Box 269
Cambridge, Minnesota 55008


ISBN 0-934860-95-5

*Dedicated to all those who have shared my island with me. Their fellowship and friendship have made the adventures contained in this book even more enjoyable.*

# TABLE OF CONTENTS

## *PART I*  FISHING

## *PART II*  HUNTING

# PART I

# FISHING

# INTRODUCTION
## FISHING ON
## THE LAKE OF
## THE WOODS

My father, Richard Lund, was a great story teller — particularly when it came to fishing and hunting adventures. When I was a child, my favorite stories were those that took place on the Lake of the Woods — long before I was born — when he and his brother Allen and the Green brothers (George and Bert) had homesteads on this most beautiful of all lakes. The year was 1912. It was a time when birchbark canoes glided among the islands and Indian villages looked very much as they had for hundreds of years.

Muskies taken in "the good old days" — The author's father, Richard Lund is second from the left.

White man's presence had been on the lake since De Noyon first paid it a visit in 1688 and the La Verendryes built Fort St. Charles in 1732. The railroad had reached Kenora in 1881 and Baudette had been a village since 1906. But Sabaskong Bay, where my father and his partners homesteaded, remained mostly untouched in the early 1900's — even by the Kenora-based loggers and miners. Thus, his fishing and hunting stories were truly of "the good old days".

It was a time when all varieties of fish seemed to compete to take a lure and record-breaking lunkers of all species haunted the waters of the Lake of the Woods. My father told of standing beneath Nestor Falls and catching northerns and muskies on almost every cast — some over 30 or even 40 pounds. Or a frog dropped in one of the deeper holes offshore was almost guaranteed to produce a walleye — frequently over 10 pounds. The biggest walleye he ever saw, by the way, came from a net and weighed twenty-one pounds!

Hunting was also incredible, although it was done for food more than for sport. The homestead was located on the east side of Hanson's Bay, near Morson, on the lakeside of the present government dock. My father and his friends had to go no farther than this bay for ducks or along its shores for partridges. Most deer were shot as they were caught swimming between islands, and moose were hunted by following shorelines in a canoe in early morning — usually in big bays like Gohere or Split Rock.

But this book isn't about the good old days; it is about the here and now. To be sure, fishing — and hunting, too — was better when my

Back in the 1930's, this 69 pounder was a world record muskie. The fisherman's name was Backus. He was from Ohio and owned The Turtle Portage Camp.

father was a young man, but some of the best hunting and fishing — anywhere — is still to be found on the Lake of the Woods. And the fish aren't out of some hatchery; they are totally wild. True, fishing isn't what it was in the "glory days" of the early 1900's, but we are now fishing for sport more than for food. It is a lot more challenging and rewarding to land and release a lunker muskie today than having one hit on nearly every cast as in my father's experience. It is more rewarding to spend the better part of a day catching enough walleyes for a good feed — with plenty of time to enjoy the scenery and good companionship — than to catch one right after the other as quickly as possible just for food. And my father did admit there were days even back then when the fish just wouldn't bite.

So here are some stories of fishing in our lifetime. I hope you will enjoy and identify with these good memories.

# CHAPTER I
## LAKE TROUT

### The Lost Colonies

It was ten o'clock on a Sunday night. I was at my home on Lake Shamineau (central Minnesota). The phone rang.

It was Neil — a frequent hunting and fishing partner. Neil and mutual friends Mark and Gene were on their way home from the Lake of the Woods — they had borrowed my island cabin for the weekend. It was the Canadian walleye opener.

"Are you still up?" Neil asked.

"Yeah — just watching the news. What's up?"

As a full blooded Scandinavian I immediately thought the worst — the guys calling that time of the night on their way home probably meant they had burned the cabin down, wrecked my boat or something worse or they would have waited 'til morning to see me at school where we all worked.

"Well, stay up," Neil advised. "We're in Motley and will be there in a few minutes."

He hung up before I could ask how bad the news was. Surely something serious had happened or they would have waited.

It was a long "few minutes", but Neil's Rambler finally pulled into the driveway. I met them under the yardlight; I just couldn't wait for them to come inside.

"Well?" I asked as the fishermen hopped out of three of the car's four doors.

Not responding, Neil popped open the trunk and he and Gene lifted out their huge, homemade cooler (it looked more like a casket) and set it down under the light.

"Are you ready for this?" Mark asked.

"No," I replied, "But this better be good this time of night; frankly, when you called I was sure you had some bad news for me."

"Nothing but good news!" Gene half-shouted as he flipped open the lid of the cooler.

At first, all I saw was bags of walleye and northern fillets showing through the chunks of ice. But the cooler was deep and I instinctively knew there had to be more — and then I saw the tail of a huge fish curled up against one end of the cooler. No — there were two tails — two big fish! They surely weren't walleyes or bass — maybe northerns, I thought. Then, as Neil unpacked the ice and bags of fillets I suddenly knew — they were lake trout!

With great ceremony, Mark laid them side by side on the lawn. They were bigger than any lake trout we had ever caught on the Lake of the Woods — well over twenty pounds each (actually 26 and 24).

Our first Whitefish Bay lunker trout.

"Where did you get them? I thought you went walleye fishing."

"We did," Gene replied, "That's how we got them."

"You were in Whitefish Bay then?" I asked.

"Yes," Mark volunteered. "But we were fishing about five miles from where we ever saw anybody fishing lake trout. We were trolling between two islands. They were about a block apart so rather than reeling in we just trolled a little faster to the second island. About halfway there Gene tied into the bigger one."

My questions poured out: "Exactly where did you get them? Who caught the other one? What were you using for bait? How deep was it?"

I can't remember who said what, but I locked the answers into my mental data bank forever:

"Neil caught the second fish."

"Mark lost a bigger one than either of these."

"Canadian Wigglers — nickel plated."

"About 30 foot of water."

"We were fishing in a bay, on the east side of . . .CENSORED! . . ."

Later, they explained that their depthfinder had revealed they had been fishing the shallower side of a 15 foot bar that ran most of the way between the two islands. The deeper side — towards the open water — was more like 50 feet deep.

They had caught the fish just before they had to come home, so there had been no opportunity to revisit the site or explore further.

As it dawned on me that I would be heading for the Lake of the Woods that next Friday afternoon, my heart began to beat faster — much faster. I really believed I must have been close to hyperventilating with excitement and anticipation.

## The Next Weekend

That next Friday marked the beginning of Memorial Day weekend. It meant an annual walleye trip for me and three other school employees: Mike, the Director of the Staples Technical College; Elmer, who taught a course in farm mechanics; and Meyer, a high school social studies teacher. I was Superintendent of Schools.

The third weekend in May, when the lost colony of lake trout had been found, was already late in the spring for the fish to be in shallow water. It was really unlikely the trout would still be around 6 days later. I cussed every warm day that week, Monday through Friday. As we finally headed north after the last day of school, we mournfully observed that the leaves on the trees were very nearly full-size. When we hit Baudette just before sundown and found the lilacs in full bloom, we admitted to each other there was little chance we'd find the trout in such shallow water so late in the spring.

Without saying so I was resigned to waiting a whole year to catch one of those big trout.

The afterglow of sunset lighted our way from Morson to my island, south of Turtle Lake, and we were able to open the cabin and unpack the boat before total darkness set in.

We had agreed the sooner we tried for lake trout the better chance we would have of hooking a straggler, so after an earlier than usual breakfast we headed north through Turtle Lake into Whitefish Bay. Neil had circled the location of the big trout on my map and we wasted no time finding the two islands and gearing up with our nickel-plated Canadian Wigglers. Gene had said they tied their lures directly to their monofilament — no leader — so we did the same.

Carefully, we retraced the route of our friends from "island one" to "island two" at slightly faster than walleye trolling speed as they had directed. The tension was enormous. No one spoke a word. But nothing. Not a strike. Nothing.

We reversed our course and trolled from the second island to the first. Still not a strike. After several runs at varying speeds we used our depthfinder to explore the other, deeper side of the bar and all water in the area of 30 to 40 foot depth. Still no action. Occasionally, fish showed up on our flasher but we had no way of knowing what they were. It was nearly eleven o'clock when someone observed, "No use — let's try for walleyes back in Sabaskong."

I reminded the guys that our friends had caught their trout in the afternoon and suggested we come back then. All agreed.

After a quick lunch on the island, we headed for one of our favorite springtime haunts — Burroagh Bay. We changed to lighter tackle — 8 pound test monofilament and jigs — tipped with half a crawler. It was our custom to try a different color jig each and then switch to whichever turned out to be the favorite. That day it was fluorescent green — Meyer's first choice. Spring walleye fishing on the Lake of the Woods is usually quite dependable, and that afternoon was no exception. We had our boat limit of 18 by three o'clock. Nice fish — averaging a little under two pounds (the size most fishermen call "three pounders" if they don't weigh them!).

As Mike brought the last walleye to Elmer's net, I asked, "Well, shall we try lake trout — or would you rather look for northerns?"

We agreed to try for trout, but not with a lot of enthusiasm. We stopped briefly at the island to freshen our thermoses with hot coffee and then headed north, arriving at the trout hole a little later than we had planned — about 4:30.

The anxiousness, the tension, and most of the hope were gone as we rather nonchalantly began trolling. Two-thirds of the way across, Mike blurted out — but a bit hesitantly as though believing it could not be a fish, "I've got something — could be bottom." Just then, the rod tip throbbed.

Someone yelled, "It's a fish!"

Another said, "Set the hook, Mike!"

Mike did set the hook and the fish took off — the handle on his closed-face Zebco reel in a free spin. Mike always uses a Zebco and Mike always doctors the drag so it won't work!

The fish took a good twenty yards of line before Mike could turn it. It seemed like a half-hour but it was probably more like ten minutes before the fish showed itself, and when it did, it was deep — right below the boat. The clear water of Whitefish Bay magnified the monster and all aboard uttered appropriate exclamations, like:

"Wow!",

"Uff da!" and

"Holy mackerel!"

It was Mike who said, laughingly, "No, it's not a mackerel; it's a lake trout."

But the trout didn't like the looks of the boat and the ugly faces looking over the side and took off on another long run. Carefully Mike brought the fish back, only to have it run again. This was repeated several times — we never could agree afterwards how many times — until Mike stole a quick glance at me and said, "I think it's ready for the net."

I really hate it when someone designates me as the netter; more than once I've lost someone's "fish of a lifetime". But this time the story had a happy ending and as Mike led the beast headfirst towards my waiting net I met him halfway and scooped the flopping trophy into the boat.

After a good deal of backslapping and handshaking, we began guessing its weight; our estimates ran from twenty-five to thirty pounds. But, as usual, fish always seem bigger when they are first caught. Back at camp, Mike's trophy weighed in at a strong twenty-three pounds.

A couple of quick photos and the trout was strung on a heavy-duty stringer and tied over the side. Trolling was resumed.

Three passes later, just when I was sure Mike had caught the last trout in the hole, it was my turn. I had never caught a lake trout over fourteen pounds, and the experience was unbelievable! It ran all the way to the end of the line and all I could do was hold my rod tip high, hang on, and pray. It was minutes before I was able to get enough line on the spool so the reel would function. When I had brought the trout most of the way in, it rolled on the surface — about 30 feet from the boat. We agreed it was bigger than Mike's.

More minutes passed and I just couldn't bring the fish near enough to net it without putting too much stress on the line. Meyer suggested that the idling outboard might be scaring it. We killed the motor, and sure enough the fish came right in. I'm not sure it was the motor or if the fish suddenly tired, but the same strategy has worked for us since on big fish. I was worried about our net, however. The mesh was old and even torn in spots. It had held Mike's fish but I believed mine to be bigger. As I asked Mike to get the net ready, I also requested of Elmer, "Pick up the other net; we might need it for backup. When Mike lifts the fish out of the water, try to get your net underneath."

My worries were justified. As Mike lifted the fish, the mesh didn't give but the aluminum handle bent. Luckily Elmer was under the trout and together they brought it into the boat!

I was sure my trout would top 30 pounds, but back in camp it weighed twenty-five — but still big enough to be a wall-hanger.

There was no more trout action that day, but Sunday morning Meyer caught his 20 pounder. He was sure he had bottom and was appropriately embarrassed when, after I had backed up, his line suddenly started moving away from the boat as he tried to pump his lure loose from the "rocks"!

We revisited the trout hole Monday morning. Just as we began to troll it began to rain, hard. "Millions" of insects — pine flies — took off from the trees. Many were driven onto the lake's quiet surface by the falling rain. We were then treated to a spectacle none of us shall ever forget. Small fish, probably tulipees, rose to take the flies, and then lake trout — big lake trout — began rolling on the surface, probably after the tulipees rather than the flies. There must have been 30 to 40 trout that surfaced over about a one-acre area!

Imagine our excitement. We tried trolling through the action —no luck; we obviously spooked them. Then someone suggested making a circle so that the lures would not follow the path of the boat. We tried the maneuver and held our rod tips high. I tied into a fourteen pounder. By the time we had boated the fish, the rain stopped, and so did the action. Another hour of fruitless trolling, trying to get Elmer his trout, ended our trip. It was so frustrating, knowing the fish were there.

Since the discovery of this lost colony of lake trout we have visited and revisited the secret spot a hundred times or more. The most we caught in any one year was eight; a couple of years we caught none. The fourteen pounder of my first trip has been the smallest; except for a nine pounder my friend, Gordie, caught on a rusty, old bucktail that would fool no respectable trout! It remains a mystery that nearly all of the fish have been over 18 pounds.

Our experiences that first year marked the beginning of a search of every nook and cranny of Whitefish Bay that held promise of holding a lake trout. We poured over charts and marked every area that had similar depth and structure to our secret hole. I don't know how many hours or days we have invested in this detective work, and although it has not been extraordinarily fruitful, it has been loads of fun and well worth the effort. Friend Ron, a St. Cloud attorney, landed an 18 pounder in a remote bay about five miles from the lost colony and about equally far from traditional trout water, but further visits to this area have been fruitless. The really good find, however, was a spot — again a long way from traditional trout water — where four of us in one weekend each caught a trophy. Mine was the first and the smallest — 26 pounds. Frequent hunting and fishing partners, Jerry (St. Cloud) and Gordie (Staples), each caught a 28 pounder. Kev (Big Lake), the youngest member of our group, caught the last and the largest. It was his first lake trout — 33 pounds!

There was one other trout adventure I must describe. My partners in the boat were Stan, Gene, and Neil — all of Staples. We caught only one trout that trip and it hit just as we were about to give up and try for walleyes. As I set the hook, the fish took off. The drag on my Garcia was set way too strong, but fortunately I had 20 pound monofilament. The power and lightning fast run of the fish bent the bale of my open-face reel straight out (something that has never happened before or since). With considerable fumbling — not knowing at first what had happened — I finally pressed my thumb on the "mono" and held it against the cork above the reel-seat to slow the fish down, but it still went to the end of the line. I held my rod tip high and the monofilament held. The fish turned and ran parallel to the boat — 100 yards out. When I tried to bend the bale back in position, it broke.

"What shall I do?" I pleaded for advice.

Neil was the first to be helpful. "I've got a spare reel in my tackle box." He responded.

Quickly he stripped all the line off his reel — it was soon all over the bottom of the boat.

"Stan, grab my line," I requested, "I'm going to cut it where it's tied to the reel."

Stan complied, holding his hand above his head for leverage and keeping the line snug. He actually began bringing the fish a little closer to the boat, but the line he had retrieved somehow tangled with Neil's line and a little branch that previously had been unnoticed on the floor of the boat. Gene came to the rescue and somehow untangled the mess. With trembling hands I finally threaded the monofilament through the eyes of my rod and tied it to the new reel.

Stan apparently had taken most of the fight out of the fish and it wasn't long before the big trout came alongside. But now there was another problem. We had left our big net back at camp and there was no way the little rubber walleye net would do the job. But we did have a gaff. Neil caught the trout under the gills first try and hoisted it aboard. It weighed just a hair over 25 pounds. After all that trouble we had to conclude the fish was just meant to be caught.

The big four. The author's was the smallest. Gordie Dezell, Kevin Crocker, and Jerry Hayenga.

Kev's 33 pounder looks even bigger mounted.

**Here's a teaser:**

*Are there any lake trout in the Lake of the Woods outside of Whitefish Bay?*

Yes.

## So What Have I Learned About Lake Trout over these Years?

● Exploring and patience pay off; I don't know which is the more important.

● Trout are unpredictable, but the sooner you can fish after ice-out the better (for shallow water fishing).

● Weather can be a factor, particularly in spring fishing. I prefer windy — even stormy — days. We have done well in sunshine, but seldom on quiet water. Wave action is helpful.

● Shiny lures work best for trolling. My favorites (naturally) are the lures I manufacture and sell myself (Dr. Lund's Little Swede, Dr. Lund's Swedish Fliver spoon, and the Big Swede).[1] Fluorescent orange (top side only) is my favorite color. My second choice has both sides nickel-plated.

● In the spring we've had our best luck trolling in 25 to 35 feet of water over large flat areas. Occasionally, we've done well on the lower edge of drop-offs. Trout may be found in 10-15 feet of water very early in the morning — just after daybreak.

● Vary the depth and speed when trolling. Trout often hit just as you speed up. Even in the spring, trout may be suspended, so try different depths. Our experience, however, has been that we have had our best luck just off bottom.

● In summer when the trout are deep, use down-riggers or hold the boat still and jig in water of 70 feet or deeper. Use a heavy jig (1 ounce to 4 ounces) tipped with natural bait, such as a strip of scaled sucker meat. I like to use a stinger hook with my jig and attach the sucker meat to both hooks.

When jigging, start on the bottom and jig there, then wind up about a dozen quick turns of the reel. Hold that depth and jig a couple of minutes. Continue raising and jigging right up to the surface. I've caught lake trout just under the boat even in the heat of mid-summer. This technique also works well when jigging through the ice (although current law prohibits the use of natural bait on Lake of the Woods for lake trout in winter). If you don't catch trout, move.

● I still enjoy shore fishing for lake trout, but at this writing it is not legal with natural bait until late May, when it is less productive. A boat is often needed to bring the bait out to where the trout feed (30 to 40 feet of water) which is usually beyond casting range.

When shore-fishing, reel your bait in along the bottom a few feet at a time, every 15 to 20 minutes. My favorite natural baits are ciscoes or chunks of scaled sucker meat. Use only enough weight to sink the bait; usually a single split-shot will do.

● Down-riggers can be productive any time of the year. Using an electronic fish locator to determine the depth at which the fish are to be found will save a lot of wasted time.

Lake trout are truly a trophy fish. A single trout should bring as much satisfaction as limits of most other species.

[1] Lund lures are available by direct mail:
> Lund Tackle
> Box 305
> Staples, MN 56479

Kevin Crocker and Chris Longbella with some Lake of the Woods trout, more typical in size.

# CHAPTER II
## CRAPPIES

On one of my very first trips to the Canadian waters of the Lake of the Woods, a Sioux Narrows resort owner greeted our party with, "You guys hit it right this time; the crappies are really biting!"

"Big deal," one of our group muttered, "We came for walleyes."

It took a few years to appreciate the local residents' love for crappies, but I have finally come to fully understand the joy of catching those big, black slabs on light tackle and now freely admit the sweet flavor of this king of panfish out of the cold waters of the Lake of the Woods is hard to beat.

Thus it was that when I acquired my own island a top priority was to locate the crappies in that area. The earliest opportunity came that June. My frequent fishing partner, Jerry, was about to be married; I would be his "best man". We had headed north for a few days of fishing before the big event. We were a little surprised that his bride, Betsy, actually encouraged the trip. Perhaps she wanted Jerry out of the way during the final preparations. But Betsy always has been tolerant of her husband's need to spend a good deal of time out-of-doors.

The walleyes and northerns provided little challenge that trip as they came almost too easy. The northerns were still in shallow water along almost every shoreline, but especially near their spawning areas — particularly near where creeks entered the lake. They snapped viciously at almost everything we threw at them. Many were small but our log book shows that our keepers were all over five pounds.

The walleyes were equally hungry and responded well to Lazy Ikes — our favorite lure in those days — trolled over sandy shallows. And it was while walleye fishing that we actually had the thrill of the trip. Jerry had just boated our 11th walleye and the outboard was in neutral. The boat was drifting sideways, therefore, and our stringer of near limits extended out at right angles to the side of the boat. Jerry was reaching for the stringer when he stopped, paused as though checking his eyesight, and then said, "Look what's following our walleyes!"

When my eyes focused, I could hardly believe what I saw — an enormous muskie, probably over 40 pounds — with his nose just inches from the last fish. As we continued to drift, the big lunker just kept his position. In the clear water we could see every mark, distinctly. I finally remembered my lure was still out and reeled it in, carefully bringing my "Ike" between the muskie's nose and the walleye, but the fish wasn't tempted in the least. Moments later, it sank a little lower in the water, like a submerging submarine, and then passed under the boat... What a thrill just to see a fish of that size! But if he had only grabbed that walleye...

With walleyes and northerns out of the way, we decided to concentrate on finding the crappies. We had been advised that this time of year they would be found in or along the edges of dead rushes (the crop from the previous year) and off rocky points. We decided to use bamboo poles with bobbers and little shiner minnows for bait. We honestly haven't used bamboo poles for crappies for years, but they are an efficient and effective implement for exploring. An added advantage is that since you are pulling directly up to set the hook there is a better chance of hooking the fish than if you are casting with spinning tackle. And explore we did — for more than four hours off points and rush beds. We did pick up a few crappies — all off points — but either the fish were not biting or there were no schools in those locations. Then we found them. It was just off a bed of the previous year's rushes that encircled a shallow reef. On the first toss of our bobbers we each picked up a small perch. These pesky little fish had tormented us all afternoon, prompting Jerry to say, "Let's move on."

For some reason, I replied, "One more perch and we're off."

But when my bobber next moved, it was a classic crappie bite. The bobber very slowly and steadily sank beneath the surface. When I set the hook, something far bigger than a perch struck back and took off in circles.

"You got a smallmouth?" Jerry asked.

I replied by swinging a pound and a half crappie into the boat. Then the fun began. When crappies are really feeding, the action is about as fast as for any kind of fishing. By lifting the heavy slabs out of the water so far from the boat we did lose a few — but it didn't matter. They bit just about as fast as the bobbers hit the water.

There were no limits on crappies in those days, but we imposed our own limits and we quit when we thought we had forty. Actual count back at the cabin, as recorded in our log book was 42.

Over the years we have revisited this first crappie haven many times. Sometimes we've found them; more often than not we haven't, but that first discovery remains by far our most memorable crappie experience at that site.

For many of us, duck hunting and crappie fishing go together. On those days when October's bright blue weather leaves the ducks

Neil Joe Smith, Meyer Engen, and Phil Anderson with a nice bunch of "saddle blankets".

sitting wherever they spent the previous night, it is great to have crappies to turn to for excitement and to help put something in the cooler for the trip home.

Fall crappie fishing is far different than early spring. Instead of being in the shallows, they'll be found in 30 or more feet of water. A light graphite or boron rod is a must, with 4# or 6# monofilament line. Even with this light tackle, it is sometimes difficult to detect the soft touch of crappies that far down. It pays to set the hook on any bump or change in pressure. Sometimes you can tell more by watching the rod tip than by what you feel.

An electronic fish locator is truly helpful; much time is saved in finding a school. This is particularly true when the crappies are suspended between the bottom and the surface. As for lures, little jigs (1/16 oz.) seem best for this deep water fishing. A split shot will get the bait down faster. If the line tangles, push the shot down against the lead-head. Color also sometimes seems to be important. At that depth the lure should be fluorescent, white or black. Water depth affects colors. Plain yellow, for example, will appear brown at that depth, (40 feet), and white will have a blue tint. Tip the jig with a small minnow or leech. At this writing, game fish or parts thereof may not be used for bait in Ontario, so I catch a few suckers every spring, scale them, and cut them into thin strips for crappies.[1]

Winter fishing is very much like fall fishing; the crappies will be in that 30 to 40 foot range. Bobbers are not essential, but since you are allowed two lines for ice fishing[1] they do come in handy. We like to use a "plain" minnow on one line and a jig tipped with a minnow on the other. Again, a fish locator is very helpful in finding the schools and determining the proper depth.

One of our more memorable winter crappie trips was just a couple of years ago with St. Cloud friends Jerry, Roger, and Steve. In fact, we were staying at Steve's cabin near Nestor Falls. The resorts had plowed a road out a few miles. Although we had snowmobiles, we joined a dozen or so fishermen that first morning at a spot along the plowed road. Fishing was slow but fairly steady. Unfortunately, the crappies weren't much for size and we were keeping about one of three caught.

Now every psychological test or inventory I have ever taken indicates that I'm a pretty conservative guy who likes familiar territory and am not likely to try new, creative ways of doing things, so I am perfectly happy to fish or hunt where I'm having some success or have had success previously. Fortunately, most of my hunting and fishing partners are just the opposite and love to explore — even when they know where they can catch fish or shoot ducks. They are always looking for something better. So this particular morning I wasn't surprised when Jerry said, "Too slow and too small — let's explore."

Nor was Jerry surprised when my response was, "Go ahead, I think I'll stay here awhile."

So Jerry and Steve headed down lake and Roger agreed to keep me company.

Roger and I continued to put a few crappies on the ice, but we had relatively little to show for our efforts at noon when we saw Jerry pulling up on his Yamaha. "Let's go have lunch," were his first words.

"Any luck?" Roger asked.

"Naw", Jerry lied, "Not much doing here I see either."

"Nope", I acknowledged, "Where's Steve?"

"Still exploring", Jerry answered, "Come on, pick up; let's eat."

I've known Jerry almost as long as I've fished and hunted and I knew instinctively by his tone of voice and the way he looked that something was up—more than he wanted to share with so many other fishermen

The author and Jerry Hayenga with "bonus fish" from a winter crappie expedition.

nearby.

"Good idea," I responded, and gave Roger a wink.

As soon as we picked up and got ourselves out of site around the next island. Jerry braked to a stop. He stepped back to his trailer sled where he dumped a six pound walleye out of a gunny sack.

"Wow!" Roger responded.

"Yeah, great fish," I acknowledged, then added, "Did you interrupt our fishing just to show us one fish?"

"Oh, no," Jerry replied, "The walleye was an accident. We've found some really nice crappies. Let's make some sandwiches, fill our thermoses, and head back to Steve."

And so we did, but we went another way around a couple of islands to avoid the other fishermen. (Once in awhile I'm *almost* ashamed of how secretive my friends and I can be when it comes to hunting and fishing.) We found Steve with a near limit of nice crappies, averaging a pound or better. Jerry had augered extra holes before coming for us; all we had to do was adjust to Steve's depth, (32 feet), and bait-up. What a fun afternoon! Many times we each had doubles or couldn't get a second line back down the hole for many minutes.

Jerry, still the explorer at heart, observed, "We don't have all that many minnows; I'm going to jig with one of your Little Swedes; maybe I can get a few walleyes."

And he had a ball. By the time we filled out our limits, Jerry had caught 15 fish on the Little Swede — without bait. Five were fairly decent walleyes — including a 3 pounder — and ten were enormous crappies, the kind my Texas friend, Neil Joe, calls "saddle blankets".

What a day! But there's one more chapter to the story. We had pulled up in front of Steve's cabin just as the sun was going down.

"I'm going to try for a walleye before dark," Roger announced, and he promptly cut a hole and lowered a Little Swede. We unpacked our sleds and were heading up the steps to the cabin when we heard Roger yell, "Hey you guys — I need help! I've really got a big one!"

We hurried to the rescue as Roger explained, "It's really big whatever it is. I can get it off the bottom, but then it just goes back down and sits there."

Jerry grabbed a chisel, standing ready to enlarge the hole if necessary.

"Has it run at all?" Steve asked.

"No, not really," Roger replied — once again coaxing the monster up a few feet, and then added, "It's pulling too hard — gotta let it go back down."

"Roger, I hate to tell you this," Steve paused to choose the right words, "But I know exactly what you've got — you've caught my telephone cable; it comes in here from across the bay!"

Whenever the four of us get together and reminisce and this particular crappie trip comes up, Roger knows — sooner or later — he'll be teased about his call for help.

## What I Have Learned Over the Years About Crappies

● Shortly after ice-out until early June, crappies may be found in the shallows, often in or near beds or rushes or off rocky points. A little later they will be found in shallow bays or around "live" beaver houses or trees that have fallen in the water.

● Fall and winter crappies will be in relatively deep water, usually between 30 and 40 feet.

● In spring or early summer, small minnows or leeches make an excellent bait. Use small bobbers; the long and narrow ones with little water resistance are better than round bobbers.

● For fall or winter fishing, small (1/16 oz.) jigs tipped with a small minnow are hard to beat. In deep water, use fluorescent colors or black or white.

● Bobbers make sense in winter when you can use two lines,[2] but they are less than helpful in the fall when a moving boat will result in changing depths. When using bobbers, jig them frequently.

● The lighter the monofilament the better — 4# is good — unless the crappies are in a feeding frenzy.

● For fall fishing, use a light, sensitive rod. Set the hook when you feel any bump or pressure.

● An electronic fish locator is a must for fall or even winter fishing. Not only will it help locate the schools, but it will also tell you at what depth to fish, particularly if they are suspended.

● We have rarely found the need for commercial fish scents when fishing the Lake of the Woods, but I have seen them work, particularly when the fish are lethargic. If your locator shows fish on the screen and they don't bite, try scent.

[1] Legal at this writing. Check current laws.
[2] Legal at this writing.

# CHAPTER III
## SMALLMOUTH BASS

### Freshwater Acrobat

Three of the biggest smallmouths I have ever caught came within a time period of about one hour; they weighed in at $5\frac{1}{4}$ pounds, 6 pounds even, and 7 pounds, 3 ounces. The last weight is the most precise because the fish was weighed in on a butcher scale in the Morson Shopping Center to qualify for an Ontario fishing contest — and it was a winner. This is how it came about.

For several years we had been walking back in to Kiwakimik (Butterfly) Lake on the Alneau Peninsula to cast for smallmouths and northerns and to enjoy the lake's pristine beauty. "If only we had a boat in here . . ." we often wished.

After one such trip when we had once again experienced the mixed emotions of elation over catching some nice northerns and smallmouths and frustration with not being able to cover more area I asked my partners of the day, "If I buy an aluminum boat will you guys help me get it back in here?"

"Yeah."

"Sure!" were the quick responses.

With those commitments, I picked up a good used boat before our next trip to the Lake of the Woods. My luckless partners in the adventure that followed were Jerry and Harry, friends and hunting and fishing partners from St. Cloud. I say "luckless" because lugging the boat plus a three-horse motor and our tackle over the half-mile or so of rocks, ridges, hummocks, and mud was anything but fun and because their fishing rewards this particular trip were nil. The only break we had on the way in was thanks to some beaver which had dammed a small stream (We used the original portage, not the shorter, higher route used today). A small meadow had been flooded, forming a little lake about a half-block across and it was certainly a lot easier paddling than walking and carrying our heavy and awkward loads. To add to our displeasure, it began to rain, and whenever it would let up the mosquitoes came out in force.

In spite of the weather, when we finally reached the lake we were still determined to fish. At least on the water we would be away from the mosquitoes.

I should explain that this particular venture was back in the early days of jig fishing, and that's what we used for bait. Our favorite was a 3/8 ounce homemade lure. We bought the hooks but poured and painted the lead heads ourselves. On cold winter evenings instead of "just" watching television we would tie on yellow maribu hair. We told

A pleasantly-heavy load of smallmouths.

A nice string of smallmouths.

spouses and unsuspecting friends that the hair came from feathers taken from the armpits of ostriches! At first we didn't add bait to the jigs, so the feathers were important. Jigs are still my favorite all-around lure but now we have replaced the feathers with minnows, leeches, crawlers, or strips of sucker meat. Also, I have this theory that fish get accustomed to lures and learn to ignore them, so we use different varieties of jigs — trying different colors, shapes, adding twister tails, using fat bodies, adding propellers, etc. But at the time of this story we were still using the unbaited, feathered jigs.

The faithful three-horse Johnson started easily, none the worse for its sometimes bumpy ride over the portage. I manned the motor and we began to troll. We hadn't proceeded 50 yards when the first bass hit my jig and exploded out of the water. "It's a nice one," Jerry observed.

I was using fairly light tackle and the fight must have taken a good 15 or 20 minutes. The fish seemed to be out of the water about as much as it was in. Each time it broke the surface I applied more pressure, making it harder for the fish to throw the hook. I remember being a tired fisherman when the bronzeback finally came to net. Our De-liar registered 5¼ pounds. The markings on all varieties of fish from Kiwakimik are particularly vivid. This fish was no exception; it was a nice trophy.

Without a moment's rest, we resumed trolling. I remember commenting that the next fish hit on the very first jig of my lure. It was even larger than the first. There were more runs, more acrobatics, more

whines of the drag, but this fish too eventually came to net and the De-liar went down to 6 pounds even. With appropriate "ooohs" and "ahhhs" we added it to our stringer and again resumed trolling. Of course there were appropriate comments from my partners like:

"Leave your line in the boat; give us a chance!" and "Do that again and I'll accidentally step on your rod!"

The three big ones from Kiwakimik Lake.

Unbelievably, it happened all over again. We had just gotten underway when fish #3 hit. But it performed differently — no acrobatics — just a hard, steady pull, more like a big walleye. I remember to this day how hard it fought and how the muscles in my forearms literally ached. At least 15 minutes went by without our seeing the fish; I was starting to think I had on a nice northern. It was almost to the boat when the bass finally took to the air, actually throwing water in my face!

"What a monster!" Harry exclaimed.

Jerry has never lost a fish for me and this one was no exception; he captured this beauty on the first pass of his net. The De-liar said 7¼ pounds!

And then it was over. Not another strike; not another fish. But what a remarkable experience; what a great memory — at least for me!

Another of my favorite smallmouth memories occurred on an early morning trip on Whitefish Bay with Jerry, long-time friend and then Minnesota Governor, Al Quie, and Al's son, Ben. We had limited out on walleyes and saved a few hefty northerns, and had even released a respectable muskie. It would be our last morning of fishing for that particular trip and the night before I suggested we try for smallmouths the next day.

"Let's get up early," Al added, "We can take the pontoon boat and I'll fix breakfast out on the lake."

Having a governor cook for us was too good an offer to pass up, so sunrise found us anchored off a sunken island in Whitefish Bay, fishing with bobbers and leeches. It was a glorious morning made even more memorable by a big bottomless pot of fresh coffee and a breakfast of ham, eggs, and fried potatoes. We even had toast made on a wire-like contraption perched on top of our Coleman stove. And the fish cooperated. When the action finally slowed down we anchored off several small islands with rocky shores (small rocks — the size of eggs or smaller). We continued to use bobbers and leeches and continued to catch fish. Al caught the largest — nearly 5 pounds. Otherwise, nothing big, just nice fish. The morning was a capstone to a very special fishing trip.

Of course, there are many other special smallmouth memories, like —

● The time we were winter fishing and Chad, (Staples), had forgotten his depth-finder. So he improvised one out of three small bell sinkers and a paper clip. He lowered the device on a bare hook — no bait — and caught a nice "smallie" — our first ever through the ice! He dropped the contraption back down (still baitless) and promptly caught two more!

● When the smallmouths went wild and Chad, Jeff, (Bertha), and George, (Scottsdale), and I released most of about 40 fish caught in less than an hour. (leeches — on the bottom — a rocky shelf — fairly shallow water).

- Opening of walleye season two years ago when we discovered a large school of smallmouths under a leaning tree. Six of us — Gordie and I from Staples and Jerry, Steve, Greg, and Roger from St. Cloud — filled out in about one hour — and they were nice fish.
- And this past spring when nephew Eric, (Brainerd), and I were trying to locate crappies, using bobbers and leeches, and he came up with three beautiful smallmouths and a nice northern instead.

### What About Largemouths?

Yes, there are largemouth bass in Lake of the Woods. The nicest ones come out of Whitefish Bay. We've caught a few in Turtle Lake. They are usually to be found in traditional largemouth water — rushes and weedbeds. Only once have we limited out on largemouths; I was with Dr. Chris — we used leeches. They seem to be increasing in numbers.

Peter Lund's smile says it all!

Eric's "bonus fish", caught while fishing crappies.

## What I Have Learned Over the Years About Smallmouth Bass

● I was surprised to learn while researching an article for *In-Fisherman* magazine that smallmouths are not native to the Lake of the Woods or even to northern Minnesota or the Boundary Waters. In the case of the Lake of the Woods, several barrels of smallmouth fry were on a train bound for a western destination. The train broke down in Kenora and there was concern the tiny fish would die — so they dumped them into the Lake of the Woods!

Logging camp cooks are credited with stocking other northern lakes; they wanted to bolster the supply of fish for their hungry lumberjacks.

● Smallmouths will take minnows, crawlers, and a great variety of artificial lures, but they *love* leeches.

● They frequent rocky shores with stones the size of eggs or smaller. They also inhabit reefs and rushes.

● Smallmouths are especially active during spawning time (June) and may be found then off rocky points, in fairly shallow water.

● It is great fun working shorelines with light tackle and small lures. Among my favorites are the smaller Shadraps, Bass Orenos, and spinner baits. Although bass seem to prefer the smaller baits, they will occasionally hit larger lures; I caught my biggest smallmouth ever, on a seven-inch muskie plug.

# CHAPTER IV
## WALLEYES

Have you ever caught a limit of walleyes, each over five pounds? I have — once — but not on the Lake of the Woods. But a young friend from Ghana, Africa, experienced this remarkable achievement the very first time he fished with hook and line on his very first trip to the Lake of the Woods!

Seth was a student in our technical college and lived with my good friends and neighbors, Stan and Rose. Seth had never fished, except with a net in Ghana, and he had never been in Canada — so I invited him to join me and my uncle Verner from Brainerd and my cousin's husband, George, from Scottsdale for a long weekend at my island.

Seth is a delightful young man and a joy to be with. He bubbles with optimism and enthusiasm. Everything was new for him on this trip and he just couldn't stop asking questions or exclaiming over each new experience.

The first evening we trolled for walleyes up in Stevens Bay off a sandy shore. It was late June. Apparently the walleyes had moved out on the reefs because there was very little action. George, Verner, and I each picked up "a keeper size" walleye, but that was it. We were just about ready to head in and I had already killed the trolling motor and started the 90 horse — slipping it into gear as the fishermen brought their lures into the boat. Seth, however, was still reeling in his rapala. The increased speed provided too much temptation for a 7-pound northern and it hit Seth's lure like a barracuda! Seth yelped. He was so excited! He was also all thumbs and just didn't seem to hear all the advice he was getting from his three coaches. But luck is with beginners and somehow he did bring the fish within reach of my landing net. Of course, compared to our little walleyes, the northern looked like a monster to Seth. He was so proud and teased us about our "minnows" far into the night.

Seth Ashiama and Uncle Verner Anderson with the record stringer.

The author's father, Richard Lund with a stringer of "just-the-right-size" walleyes.

The author with an "almost nine pounder".

The next morning I suggested trying Whitefish Bay for walleyes.

"Walleyes?" Seth asked incredulously, "Why fish walleyes when you can catch northerns?"

I tried to explain how good walleyes tasted and so on — but I'm sure Seth wasn't convinced. He did feel better, however, when I assured him we'd try for northerns after we caught some walleyes.

We anchored the boat on the edge of a sunken island, about an acre in area and with a depth varying between 6 and 12 feet. It was surrounded by much deeper water — well over 50 feet deep. We used

Governor Al Quie and son, Ben, with the fruits of a good morning's labor.

slip bobbers and leeches and let the light breeze carry our bait over the shallow area. Seth's bobber hadn't been in the water five minutes when it slowly submerged. He counted to ten as coached and set the hook. I had set his drag fairly light so he wouldn't break the line and as a result we didn't see the fish for about 15 minutes. Seth was convinced he had a northern. I wasn't so sure he wasn't right — but when the fish finally appeared in the clear water about 6 feet below the boat we saw that it was a beautiful walleye. Moments later it registered 7 pounds on our De-liar!

Seth was so pleased there was no way I was going to explain that we usually let the bigger walleyes go. But it was because of that reluctance that we ended up with the nicest stringer of walleyes I have ever seen on that part of the Lake of the Woods. Of course, as soon as Seth landed the first walleye he wanted to cast for northerns, but I insisted, "Not until you catch your limit of 6 walleyes."

The rest of our story is even more unbelievable. The fish seemed to like Seth's bait and only Seth's bait. In the next couple of hours Seth caught five more walleyes — all over 5 pounds! We three experienced fishermen never caught a single walleye.

As I netted Seth's sixth walleye, he asked, "Now can I cast for northerns?"

"Sure," I replied, (What else could I say?) I snapped one of my Fliver Spoons on his line. On his *first cast,* just as Seth was about to lift the spoon out of the water, a 5-pound northern hit. He was using a close-faced reel and somehow the monofilament looped around the handle. But that didn't bother Seth. A muscular, well built kid, he just pulled back with all his might and the northern came sailing through the air, hitting Uncle Verner in the back of the head, knocking his glasses into his lap and his hat into the water!

The blow to the head seemed to change Verner's luck and he picked up two walleyes, but neither made the 5-pound mark.

Although we all tried, I really don't think we were able to convince Seth that he had experienced the fishing trip of a lifetime.

My friends Gordie and Russ and I have had many a memorable opening weekend for walleyes together. One such weekend stands out not only because of our success but because of what we learned about early season walleyes.

The opening Saturday that year had been a very long day. The lake was flat calm, the sky cloudless, and the temperature in the unseasonable eighties. Catching walleyes under those conditions is a real challenge and we didn't prove up to it. We tried every trick in the book. We trolled; we jigged; we used minnows, leeches, and crawlers and a variety of artificial lures. Eight hours on the lake yielded four unimpressive walleyes. When we went in for supper, we decided to stay in until just before dark and then give it another try.

While enjoying our after-dinner coffee, Russ had an idea: "I remember reading in *In-Fisherman* magazine that early season walleyes sometimes come into sandy shallows just before dark, looking for minnows attracted by the warmer water."

"The Isle of the East Wind (we named it that because fishing was at its best there with an east wind) has a long, shallow point. Maybe we should try that," Gordie suggested.

Having no better idea, we pushed off in the Tyee just before sunset and headed west. The 15-minute ride was once again on a calm lake. We anchored close to shore in about 3 feet of water. We had discussed our strategy on the way out and decided to use minnows with slip bobbers. The area into which we would be casting checked out at 5 to 6 feet deep. The sun dipped below the horizon and it started to get dark, but there was no action — nothing — not even a perch bite.

When the fish aren't hitting, Gordie loves to experiment. Without saying a word, he cranked in his bobber and replaced his equipment with a featherless green jig and hooked on the minnow he had been using. He made a long cast — out from shore. He let the lure settle to the bottom and then began a slow, jerky retrieve — letting the jig occasionally hit bottom and stir up the sand. About halfway in we saw Gordie set his hook. "I've got one!" He half-shouted.

Adam Clabots with the results of his very first evening on The Lake of the Woods.

But seconds later, he reported, "Lost it."

Gordie's lure was almost to the boat when he yelped, "Got another one!"

This time it stayed on and he boated a fat, 2-pound walleye. And so began some of the finest, fastest walleye fishing I have ever experienced. By the time Russ and I had changed to jigs Gordie had two more fish in the boat. Each of us had action on nearly every cast. Frequently we would miss a strike or lose a fish, but no problem — as with Gordie's first cast, another would hit the jig-minnow combination on the way in. Sometimes we even lost the second fish and got a third! The feeding frenzy continued into total darkness as we filled out the day's limit — all decent fish. Some of the walleyes must have struck in no more than 3 to 4 feet of water. It was great fun and an educational experience that has meant several successful early season trips in recent years (and not just on the Lake of the Woods).

Five "peas in a pod" from the same hatch.

Oh, I did forget to mention one little detail. Gordie and I have had a long-running argument centering around the advantages and disadvantages of closed vs. open-faced reels. Somehow, the monofilament on my open face became hopelessly entangled in the near darkness that night and as a result I missed out on the final action. I still hear about that!

There are many, many good memories about fishing walleyes through the ice on the Lake of the Woods — most of them involving snowmobiling to my island. And I have had some good winter trips on the Minnesota side of the lake — usually out of resorts at or near the mouth of the Rainy River. As I get older, I'm becoming softer and must admit I don't mind being pampered at a resort with warm beds, good food, and a trip to a preheated fish house in a Bombardier or van-on-tracks.

On one such trip with Dr. Chris (we were celebrating his recently acquired M.D. degree) we compromised on comfort and opted to spend a night in one of Wigwam Lodge's larger houses, equipped with bunks and a gas plate to cook on. The Bombardier dropped us off shortly after daylight.

"There's really no hurry," the driver advised, "they don't bite much before 9 o'clock."

He left us with a generous supply of minnows and some more advice: "Only thing to use is a fluorescent jig — purple or green — baited with a minnow."

I'm usually a good soldier so I rigged up as ordered. Chris, on the other hand, is more of a maverick — always experimenting — and it seems to pay off for him. For example, I still haven't forgotten our trip to Goose Bay, Labrador, for brook trout. I used flies and Mepps spinners as suggested by our guide. Chris used one of my Little Swedes

Dan Lund with his first winter walleye.

(gold finish) and caught half-again as many trout as I — several between 3 and 4 pounds.

So this time, Chris announced, "I'm just going to use plain minnows on both my lines. That way I can do other things."

"Other things like what?" I asked.

"Like make coffee, read, and cook your meals," he replied.

Yeah, you guessed it, Chris outfished me — badly — and I sat there jigging my arm off all day. We caught nearly all saugers, but I really think they are "saug-eyes" (part walleyes) because they are much lighter colored and rounder than saugers found elsewhere in the lake — and usually a little larger.

The action stopped at dark, so we had a dinner of pan-fried saugers and relaxed for a good visit, turning in early. I don't know if the bunks were all that good, but I recall sleeping well — I was probably worn out from all that jigging.

The next day dawned bright and clear and unseasonably warm. We decided to open four holes outside the house and enjoy the nice weather. This time I used plain minnows in both holes. So what did Chris do? He switched to one of my Little Swedes — baited with a minnow. Do I have to tell you what happened?

I suppose I could fill a book with walleye stories. I've said nothing about jig-fishing on reefs — my favorite way to catch walleyes — or jigging in deep holes (20-30 feet) in autumn. One of the greatest sensations known to freshwater fishermen is setting that jig — directly below the boat — into a solid walleye.

I can't close this chapter without mentioning my old friend and mentor, Don Hester, (Cass Lake). He has taught me so many things about both fishing and hunting, like: baited jigs without feathers are more productive than feathered baited jigs — and it's wiser to watch what early-morning bluebills are doing rather than setting up decoys where you think they will be and then having to pick up and move. Over the years we have fished together from Leech Lake to Great Bear, Great Slave, and the Tree River, and we've hunted deer, caribou, and moose from Ontario to Alaska.

One of my good memories is Don's teaching me about fishing weedbeds for walleyes — either along the edge of thick weeds or in among scattered weeds. That lesson came on an August trip to Miles Bay with Don and his buddy since high school days, "Red" (St. Cloud). Don chose a small, weedy bay south of Garden Island. He suggested we use "Lindys" with crawlers. As we slowly back-trolled in and on the edge of weedbeds we picked up limits of 2 to 3 pounders with black backs and golden bellies. Fish are chameleons and I suppose these walleyes took their dark colors from the thick weeds they lived in.

We still call that spot "Hester Bay". (And we have a few more Hester Bays around the lake as well!)

### What Have I Learned about Walleyes?

● Walleyes are the most predictable fish I know; therefore it pays to keep a detailed log of when and where you catch them and under what conditions and with what bait.

● Walleyes change habitat with the season. Start in May along the shorelines, usually in 8 to 12 feet of water. With warmer weather (June), move to the reefs — 6 to 16 feet. Big walleyes will sometimes be just off the reefs, in 20 or more feet of water. Try points of shorelines, or even bays, where the wind has been blowing in for some time. Don't forget the weedbeds, especially in August or early fall, but I have caught them there much earlier. With cold weather, go deeper. Through the ice, try 9 to 14 feet but they may be much deeper. Saugers will be at 20 feet or more and also on the bottom.

● If walleyes are not hitting, experiment with different lures and baits. Minnows seem more effective in spring and fall. Research shows that walleyes' favorite food in May and September is shiner minnows, and that perch are the natural food of preference in the summer months.

● Day in and day out jigs are the most productive lure, but I have seen times trolling with Rapalas or similar lures is more productive.

Lazy Ikes and similar lures baited with pieces of crawlers can be dynamite.

● When jigging through the ice, small spoons (Little Swedes or Swedish Pimples, for example) baited with minnows are usually more effective than lead jigs.

● Walleyes, more than any other fish, have color preferences. Experiment. My favorite colors, in order of preference, are fluorescent red, fluorescent orange, fluorescent green, yellow, purple, white and black. Sometimes unpainted jigs are best.

● If walleyes are not biting, change locations as well as bait. Try different depths and structure. If you don't catch a fish in 20 - 30 minutes, change locations.

● For bigger walleyes, try deeper water. Trolling deep and a little faster with down-riggers can be very productive — particularly on Big Traverse where the depths are more uniform.

Gordie Dezell and Neil Krough with a northern and a box full of winter walleyes.

# CHAPTER V
## NORTHERN PIKE

Early spring — before the walleye opener — is our favorite time of the year for fishing northerns. With today's severe limits on lake trout it is nice to have a viable alternative — another excuse to enjoy the first respite from winter. Perhaps only the glories of autumn can equal the joys of spring with its warming sun, budding birch and aspen, and crystal clear waters.

Each and every spring on the Lake of the Woods has its special memories. One such memory is from several years ago, shortly after ice-out. Nephew Bruce, old friend Don, and I had become bored with two consecutive days of very poor lake trout fishing on Whitefish Bay. You know how trout can be. They are the most temperamental and unpredictable of all freshwater fish. We tried everything from shore-fishing to trolling to jigging with only two less than average trout to show for our efforts — and that was for six fishermen! The other three members of our party had decided to stick with lake trout fishing to the end but Don, Bruce, and I had had it with trout fishing and on that second day, with only few hours of fishing time left for the trip, we wanted something to bring home. Northern pike from icy cold spring waters are mighty tasty on the table and well worth bringing home — especially now that we have learned how to debone them completely. In fact, I hear more and more fishermen confess that boneless northern is more than the equal of walleye (such heresy!).

And so it was that after wishing the other boat "good luck" we returned to Sabaskong Bay to a favorite spot at the mouth of a creek (actually the outlet of a small lake) where we suspected spawned-out, hungry northerns would be hanging around looking to pick off smaller suckers on their spawning run.

And sure enough — as we approached the outlet, even before we had turned off the motor, we could see the splashing of suckers as they encountered the shallows on their way to fulfill their sexual urge.

You may be surprised by our fishing technique. Our weapon of choice was a bobber, split shot, and very large dead shiner minnow. Experience has convinced us that in early spring northerns — especially the big ones — are more likely to take a dead shiner than chase after a spoon or other artificial lure. Besides, as a fisherman, I have never quite grown up; I still love to watch a bobber as it is pulled across the surface and gradually slips out of sight, or is pulled under with such violence that you can actually hear it "plop".

We anchored our boat off to one side of the slight current and rigged up — setting our bobbers at about three feet above the bait. We would be fishing in from five to six feet of water. The bobbers we used were streamlined and weighted so that they floated barely above the surface and could easily be pulled under without alerting the fish.

Bruce was first in — casting his minnow to the mouth of the outlet where the slight current would carry it out from shore. Before either Don or I made our initial cast he announced, "Got a bite."

Sure enough, the bobber was out of sight. Bruce counted off the last seconds, "57 — 58 — 59 — 60!" and set the hook. And then the fun began! Very few species of fish are the equal of northern pike when it comes to long, lightning runs and sheer stamina. About five minutes and five runs later I netted Bruce's nice pike; we estimated it at "seven or eight pounds".

It was one of those days when northerns were in a feeding frenzy and they provided two hours of great sport. We caught no pituitary giants but what could be more fun than catching 18 nice-size northern pike[1] so quickly?

By the time our partners returned from trout fishing we had our trophies all steaked-out, bagged and on ice — ready for the trip home. We had made the better choice — there were no additional trout. Needless to say, our friends were more than willing to share our good luck and to bring home some good eating.

Spring trips have meant some fine trophy northerns over the years — several between 18 and 24 pounds (our largest). I particularly recall a 21 pounder that led Bruce on a merry chase. We had anchored about 30 feet from a marker buoy — but not far enough. On the northern's "umpteenth" run it circled around the buoy — all the way around. We pulled anchor and gave chase and miraculously eventually landed the fine trophy that now hangs on his wall.

Nephew Bruce Lund and Don Hester with limits of nice northerns.

Another memorable northern trip was just last May. Nephew Eric and I were up to open camp and to rebuild the ramps and cribs leading to my two floating docks. We knew the work would take up most of our long weekend and we wanted to use whatever time we had for fishing for lake trout. I knew we'd have a tough time keeping our minds on our work — especially on the first open water trip of the year. So, as we planned the trip, I suggested, "I think I'll freeze some big shiners; maybe we can pick up a few northerns while we work on the dock."

Eric wasn't hard to convince, "It'll sure be a lot more fun working if we can fish at the same time. But what are our chances of getting any?" he wanted to know.

I replied that we had picked up an occasional northern early in the year under similar circumstances and thought it would be well worth the effort. I went on to say, "Years ago my dad would set a bamboo pole this time of the year and did pretty well. About half the time a northern

This one hit the author's dead shiner.

Chad Longbella with a couple of "almost trophies".

would pull the pole into the lake before he could get to it and we'd end up chasing it with the boat!"

"Sounds like fun," was Eric's reply, and so northern fishing became a part of our work plan.

Before starting on the docks, we used the boat to get our bobber-shiner combinations far enough out from shore so that the crosswind that was blowing wouldn't take them in too close.

What followed was a very ineffective work day. Oh, we finished the ramps all right, but it took more than twice as long as it should have. We spent far more time watching our bobbers, catching fish, and putting our lines back out than sawing boards or hammering nails. In other words, we had a lot of fishing action. By day's end we had 10 nice northern pike. Fortunately, only one was legal trophy size (27 1/2 inches),[2] and most of the others were "just a hair" under that size. I say "fortunately" because all too often a fish will swallow the minnow. We used 20# monofilament so we could cut the line on larger fish if we caught too many, and let them go with a good chance of survival—but I don't like doing that.

Next day, work done, we headed for Whitefish Bay. The weather, as so often happens in early spring, had turned real nasty. Although I believe trout bite better in bad weather, trolling is difficult in rough water. Now that fishing with fish or fish parts for bait is illegal in Whitefish Bay until late in May, trolling with spoons or other artificial lures is about the only option. We had a tough time fishing where we wanted to and never had a strike. When it started to rain I asked, "What do you think, Eric, should we give it up and go back to the island and try for the last two northerns we need for our limits?"

"You bet!" was his quick reply, "I'm freezing."

Upon returning to the island, we cast out from the leeward side and let the wind carry our baits out from shore. It took awhile — quite awhile — but we each caught a northern — the larger going 13 pounds. Modesty prevents me from telling you who caught it!

So what if the trout didn't bite!

In our experience, fall is the second most productive time for northerns. Usually we catch them while jigging in deep water (20 - 30 feet) for walleyes or crappies. It is our theory that they are hanging around to pick off the smaller fish. Several times we've had northerns hit walleyes or crappies while we were pulling them up — and we've even landed a few that way. Trolling the edge of crappie beds with muskie lures can produce some real lunkers — both northerns and muskies. Which reminds me of a crappie trip many years ago (so long ago it was then legal — I think — to shoot into the water to stun a big fish before landing it). One of the fellows tied into a nice northern, but didn't have a landing net. They had been duck hunting earlier in the day and someone suggested stunning the fish with a blast from a shotgun. Normally a rifle would be used but a shotgun sounded reasonable. No sooner said than done, but instead of stunning the fish it took off at breakneck speed on a world record run! Luckily the drag was set relatively light. Some crappie fishermen in another boat came to the rescue with their net and landed a fat 15 pounder.

And that reminds me of another story, told by the late Ted Rowell, Sr., of Baudette. He and former Minnesota Governor Luther Youngdahl were fishing muskies with a guide and a cameraman in Minnesota waters, making a movie to promote tourism. Ted tied into a trophy muskie and after they had enough footage on film the guide took out his revolver and shot into the water close to the muskie's head, stunning it and making it easier to boat. (Now illegal).

"If you get another one, I'd like to shoot it," the governor volunteered.

A little later Ted hooked another muskie and after the fish was played out the guide handed Youngdahl his revolver. The Governor took careful aim, holding the gun with both hands, and promptly shot the line in twain just in front of the lure!

Casting for northerns in the summer in bays or along weedbeds can be both fun and productive — especially where the wind has been blowing in. A good memory which illustrates the tenaciousness of the northern pike took place a few years back. A young man named Peter, (son of then Minnesota Education Commissioner Duane Matheies), was casting a Bassoreno at the edge of a bed of rushes. Just as he was about to lift the plug from the water, a nice northern (it turned out to be a seven pounder) struck with a violent splash and snapped the line. It was the first strike of the day for Peter and he was naturally disappointed. So I tied on a duplicate of the lure he had lost. On the very next cast he had another hit. This time we netted the fish — with his lure entangled in the hooks of the lure he had lost, anchored securely in the jaws of the fish!

Winter fishing for northerns also has its share of memories, only one of which I will share in closing this chapter. Brothers Chad and Chris and friend Kevin and I were on the lake fishing for walleyes. Fishing was excellent and we had filled out and returned to the cabin for lunch. Chad and I were in the cabin doing dishes while Chris and Kev were out front trying for northerns — using dead minnows and tip-ups. A flag suddenly popped up and both fishermen took off on the run. It would have been an interesting race because both were in college at the time and were runners on champion track teams. But Kevin had forgotten he had borrowed my overshoes (three sizes too large). As he took off, one overshoe went flying through the air, and on his second leap the other took off in the opposite direction. Kev hit the ice — plowing snow! Chris, meanwhile, landed a nice northern. Poor Kev was left to retrieve the overshoes to the riotous laughter of his three companions. If it weren't for our log book, that spectacular sight would probably have been my only memory of the trip!

**What I Have Learned About Fishing Northern Pike**

● Whether trolling or casting, relatively fast and erratic action is best. Northerns will often hit as you speed up or quicken the retrieve.

Nephew Dirk Manoukian with a winter northern.

● Dead shiners or suckers are excellent spring or winter bait. Of course, given a choice, I prefer live bait.

● In the spring of the year, just casting out a dead shiner and letting it sink to the bottom can be effective.

● Since big northerns haunt schools of crappies or even walleyes, it often pays when fishing through the ice to bait the second line you are allowed (at this writing) for northerns.

● Big northerns are often caught in deep water (except in spring). Indians told early explorers that there was a separate species of northerns that inhabit deep water. They called them "pike who live with trout". When you think of all the bait fish — such as tulipees and ciscoes — that inhabit deep water, it makes sense that northerns would be there too.

● I think northerns like color, especially red or fluorescent colors, but silver (nickel) is also effective.

[1] Prior to length limitations being enforced.

[2] At this writing only one of a limit of six may be longer than $27\frac{1}{2}$ inches.

# CHAPTER VI
## MUSKIES

I must confess at the outset that I am not a muskie hunter. I will admit that when I catch a muskie or even see one follow I momentarily lapse into muskie fever, but I have never joined the growing legions of fishermen who spend endless hours churning the waters along the shorelines and weedbeds.

The Lake of the Woods has some of the finest muskie waters on the continent and has produced several world records in various line-pound-test categories — including, at one time, the largest caught on any weight line. In fact, there are so many muskies in the lake I don't think there has ever been a year when I have not caught a nice muskie, even though it has usually been while fishing for some other species. And so I do have some great muskie memories — in spite of myself.

One of my fondest recollections is of my father catching a nice muskie from my island the first year I purchased it. In fact, it was on the second or third trip. My most frequent hunting and fishing partner, Jerry, (St. Cloud principal), and I were painting the floor of the porch of the guest cabin. My dad was painting the outside of the main cabin. I had decided to go back to that cabin (a little over a hundred foot walk) to brew some coffee. As I came over the slight rise of ground between the two cabins I saw a remarkable sight. My father was in the lake on his hands and knees and water was splashing violently all around him. Suddenly, a beautiful muskie came flying through the air and lit well up on the shore. As my father crawled out of the water and struggled to his feet, I ran to the fish and kept if from flopping back into the water.

Breathlessly, my father explained that while painting he had seen an obviously big fish swirl a few feet off shore. His rod was leaning against a tree; it was rigged with a red and white Lazy Ike. The fish hit on the first cast. Of course he had no net. So when he had finally played out the fish he waded into knee-deep water and then brought the fish into

Gordie Dezell with a 30 pound muskie.

Jeff Cowie — The smile says it all: "first muskie".

Jack Carlson weighs in a 30 lb. muskie, caught on one of his first casts, his first time on the lake.

the shallows between him and the shore. He then fell to his knees, dropped the rod, and got both hands under the fish — heaving it up on the beach. It was at that point I had come up over the rise of ground.

The muskie was not a monster, but it did weigh a little over 20 pounds. Because it was our first muskie and because it was caught from the island we had it mounted and it hangs today on the cabin wall. And we still call the spot where my dad caught it "Muskie Point".

It is always a special memory when a youngster catches a big fish. My Minnesota neighbor, Stan, and his eight year old son, Jon, and I were up fishing walleyes. Jon had done very well and when his father observed, "Jon, do you realize you've caught more than twice as many walleyes as I have?" Jon replied in all sincerity, "Gee, Dad, I'm sorry. You can land the next one I get on."

Sometime later the walleyes stopped biting and Jon asked if he could cast for northerns. "Sure," Stan replied, "But don't cast there," he said pointing at a weedbed, "You'll just get hung-up."

Jon didn't mean to disobey but his first cast landed plop in the middle of the weeds.

"Not there, Jon!" his father yelled.

Just then the water literally exploded as a nice muskie went airborne with Jon's plug in its mouth!

Jon was fishing with a 202 Zebco reel and a rod so short it only had two line-guides. But the muskie was well-hooked and the drag set just right. It seemed to take forever but we finally netted the fish.

You can imagine Jon's pride and excitement; it was by far his biggest fish ever. He began talking about bringing it home to show his mother and older sister and friends. I feared, however, it might not quite make the then legal minimum length of 40 inches. With great trepidation I took out my tape and measured from the end of the lower jaw to the tip of the tail and found that it was just a hair short. I made a snap decision and assured Jon it was big enough. I rationalized that the odds of being checked by a warden were small and it was so close. Of course, you know what happened — a gamecheck on the Canadian side of the Baudette bridge! Before the warden even had a chance to see the fish I began telling the story about Jon's first muskie. I'm sure in retrospect I over-did it; the warden had to know something was wrong. Horror of horrors, he didn't say a word but whipped out his tape. He didn't just measure it once; he measured it three times — and each time looked me straight in the eye. After the third time, he paused for effect, again looked me in the eye, winked, then turned to Jon and said, "Nice fish, son!"

Don't tell me wardens don't have a heart!

Muskies are a most improbable fish and nearly every one caught is worth a story. One of the most unlikely stories is that of Jack, (St. Cloud principal, now retired), who, on his very first trip to the Lake of the Woods and on one of his very first casts, caught the 30 pounder pictured here. I have guided three others whose *first* fish on the lake was a muskie, even though they were trying for bass or walleyes. And then there is Jim, (retired St. Cloud teacher) who caught three nice muskies the same day one fall while jigging in 20 feet of water for walleyes. And yet others may cast thousands of times before getting a strike.

Finally, my own best personal muskie memory is of one that got away. It was in very clear shallow water. The enormous fish (I really believe it may have weighed between 50 and 60 pounds) took my jig right by the boat. The fish was lengthwise, parallel to the boat, just a few inches under the surface. I can still see every mark and spot! It just inhaled the jig and slowly turned away from the boat. Of course I had no leader and a few minutes later my line just went limp as its sharp teeth severed my eight pound mono. Yet I had the thrill of seeing it so clearly and so close. That memory is *almost* as good as having the fish on the wall.

I was going to say that this was the largest freshwater fish I had ever seen — in or out of the water, but that wouldn't have been true. One summer afternoon in Whitefish Bay when the sun was just right I saw *two* larger fish. My partners were Chris, Chad and Kev. We were casting along some rushes when suddenly we were aware of two huge fish just on the other side of the rushes in shallow water. Our first thought of course was muskies. But they were too big and the shape and coloration were wrong. They looked like sharks! As they became aware of our presence and moved out in front of the boat we got a better look — sturgeon!

**What I Have Learned Over The Years About Fishing Muskies**
- Nothing!

# CHAPTER VII
## OTHER SPECIES

### Whitefish

I really wish I knew how to catch whitefish. I love to spear them through the ice in Minnesota, and even more, I love to eat them — smoked, baked, or broiled. The only whitefish we've caught on the Lake of the Woods have been in the spring and on jigs while fishing walleyes in relatively shallow water. My whitefish pictured here was $8^1/2$ pounds — and that's larger than any I have ever speared. But friend Neil caught an even larger one — 11 pounds! Interestingly, I don't think we've ever caught one under 5 pounds.

The author's $8^1/2$ pound whitefish.

## Tulipees

Along about March, the tulipees really bite well through the ice. We've often caught them in water 30-40 feet deep, but the tulipees have usually been suspended between 15 and 20 feet. Once found, they produce tremendous action and they really fight. We use a sunfish or crappie jig tipped with a mousie or waxworm.

Several years ago a bunch of us decided to catch 1000 tulipees to have smoked or pickled (like herring). We did it in a day and a half of fishing. The keepers ran between half a pound to a pound and a half. A few ran larger. In retrospect it was kind of dumb to take that many, but a whole lot of friends had some good eating. By the way, tulipees are also good filleted, cut up, poached, and dipped in melted butter.

## Eelpout

About the only time we've caught eelpout on the Lake of the Woods has been while shore fishing for lake trout or through the ice at night while fishing walleyes. But I know this — we've never thrown one back! Over the years I have seen a few walleye fillets left on the platter, but there has never been leftover eelpout!

# PART II

# HUNTING

# INTRODUCTION
## HUNTING ON
## THE LAKE OF
## THE WOODS

Hunting on the Lake of the Woods is special. I have enjoyed hunting mallards in western Minnesota in shallow sloughs; I've thrilled to the sight of flocks of geese settling into the decoys on the fields of Saskatchewan — but the pristine beauty of the Lake of the Woods provides a setting that makes the hunting experience there particularly rewarding. For example, nowhere have I found bluebill hunting that compares with setting up on a small is-

A young black lab's first bluebill.

land on the Lake of the Woods — particularly on a blustery day with a little snow in the air. That moment when you reach out to accept a fat bluebill from your Labrador retriever as it scrambles up a slippery rock and you note the delicate hues of purple and green in the drake's head as you turn your trophy in your hand — is a moment when you would like to live forever.

Or, how about those days when a howling northwest wind drives the low-lying clouds like scattered sheep across the sky, but you are snug and sheltered in a spruce and willow-lined bay waiting for the evening flight of ring bills. And when they come, they announce their arrival with a rush of air through their wings and display the speed, profile, and sound of miniature military jet planes as they take that first pass at your decoys — always just out of range.

Then there is the unique beauty of a high stand of golden wild rice through which you paddle a canoe with your partner up front anticipating that moment when a pair of mallards may explode from their hiding place as they jump straight up in front of you — camouflaged for the moment as their colors blend with the autumn leaves on the trees surrounding the rice bed.

Or, how about deer hunting on the Lake of the Woods? Where else can you climb rock ridges from where you can see forever, looking back over a lake reflecting October's bright blue sky, dotted with scores of pine-covered islands? Falling aspen leaves cling to the dew-covered needles of spruce trees below — like golden Christmas ornaments. Mesmerized by the beauty, you nearly forget why you have come.

There is only one Lake of the Woods; what a privilege to hunt and fish surrounded by its magnificence!

Nephew Steve Clabots with mallards taken before breakfast while paddling through heavy rice.

# CHAPTER I
## BLUEBILLS

Thinking back over scores of successful bluebill hunts, the one I have chosen to share first was particularly memorable because of the unusual circumstances and the reassurance it brought that there is still justice in this world.

We had been enjoying a long, but slow, four-day weekend. It was the morning of the third day — Saturday — the four of us, (my partners were Steve from St. Cloud and Gordie and Neil from Staples), had managed to scratch out a little more than half our possession limit, (16 each at that time, including our late-season bluebill bonus). There just didn't seem to be many birds around. Neil and Gordie had explored as far north as Alfred's Inlet and as far east as the end of Portage Bay. Steve and I had been as far north as Miles Bay and as far west as the Sunset Channel, but we had found no concentrations of divers anywhere. Nor were there mallards around. The locals were long-gone and the northerns were late in coming down. The ducks we had for dinner the night before had reduced our bag to exactly half our possession limit.

We finished breakfast that Saturday morning with little optimism, yet, once again, the break of day found Steve and me heading west and Gordie and Neil exploring east. Our first stop was a rockpile in Sabaskong Bay which we had named "Quincy Island". It was named for the old TV show based on the adventures of a coroner by that name — starring Jack Klugman. Several falls earlier, Neil and a hunting partner, Jack, (also a Staples vocational instructor) had a good hunt there and felt the little island deserved a name. One of them (both now take credit) observed that cormorant and sea gull droppings had killed virtually every bush and blade of grass on the rock pile and suggested "Quincy" as an appropriate name because everything — even the ducks that had been foolish enough to come into their decoys — was dead!

That Saturday morning, however, the hunting was also dead and by 11 o'clock, neither Steve nor I had fired our guns, nor had there been any birds in site — anywhere. As we emptied our first thermos, Steve observed, "I realize it's no use, but I suppose we'd better go look for some ducks."

I wasn't hard to convince, so we picked up our twenty-odd magnum decoys and agreed to head northwest, regretting that we had taken so long to make a move. Just before rounding Rabbit Point, a guide and two hunters with two 35's on the back of their boat, passed us and appeared headed for the Sunset Channel. Not anxious to follow them, we swung around Rabbit Point and headed back east.

"Can those be ducks?" Steve asked, pointing to what appeared to be a raft on the lake in the distance.

Before I could pass judgment, about a thousand bluebills lifted off the water; they circled around us and passed over the disappearing guided boat.

I suggested the point of a large island for our set-up — near where the ducks had been rafted. Steve agreed. We were only yards from the island when the guide passed us with a roar, cut his motors, and began throwing out decoys even before his boat had stopped its forward motion!

Steve and I were appalled and momentarily speechless. I finally found my tongue and asked a stupid question: "Are you guys going to hunt here?"

The guide responded with sarcasm, "What does it look like?"

I turned to the hunters, who still sat motionless side by side, and asked, "Are you going to let your guide get away with this? You knew we were going to hunt here. We found the ducks!"

One hunter looked away in embarrassment; the other shrugged his shoulders and murmured something about, "Well, he is the guide."

Meanwhile, Steve had been looking around and pointed to a much smaller island about 3 blocks away, "Let's get out of here. Let's try it over there," he suggested.

"Might as well," I responded and kicked our motor in gear.

We set-up on the sheltered side of the rocky island and pulled our boat up behind a boulder. There was little cover for a blind, but enough.

"Not an empty shotgun shell on the island," I observed, "doesn't look real promising."

But before the last words were out of my mouth a flock of bills swung in from nowhere and plopped down into our decoys! Neither of us had a shell in our Brownings.

As we loaded our guns, the flock took off, but circled and came back

Bruce Lund, son — Jack Lund, and Chad Longbella — all of Staples and the results of a good day's hunt on a rocky island. The nosy dog is Sandy, a white lab.

in! This time we were ready and three bluebills stayed behind. As Sam the Labrador dropped the first bird into my waiting hand, Steve pulled on the wing feathers. "One, two, three, four, five, six, seven — they run all the way to the tip" he observed as he counted the white feathers in the spectrum. "They're greater scaup," he announced.

"They're big and they're dumb, Steve; must have come in from the north last night."

And that was just the beginning. Sam was still on his way to the third bird when a second flock attacked the island. There must have been more than a hundred birds. They were all over — in front of us, behind us, circling, milling, lighting in the decoys.

"What are we waiting for?" Steve asked, and we both opened fire. Six shells later, one single duck lay in the water.

"How many did we get?" I asked.

"I see only one," Steve replied.

"Impossible!"

But there was only one duck. And how often that happens with a big flock.

From then on the action was steady and the shooting improved. Flocks came in all sizes — singles, doubles, triples, and small flocks sneaking in only a wing tip above the water. And then there were big flocks, too, that you could see coming for a mile. It was a glorious afternoon. Sam was in dog heaven with all the retrieving. Not a bird was lost. The dog even swam down the cripples, matching them dive for dive. I still find it unbelievable that a dog can outswim a duck underwater. One cripple was so far out we could barely see Sam's head bobbing in the waves. "I think I'd better go get him," I told Steve. But before I had both feet in the boat, Steve yelled, "He's coming back!" And he had the duck.

We couldn't help but enjoy the fact that scarcely a shot came from the guided hunters. Even when the guide took his boat out to scare up rafts of ducks that accumulated from time to time, they always came our way. "Yes," Steve observed, "There is justice in this world after all."

After downing our fourteenth bird, I told Steve, "We're going to fill out soon. I'll take a limit with me and go back for Gordie and Neil."

"Good idea," he replied, "I doubt if they've found any birds."

I left Sam with Steve and headed for my island, where I had planned to drop off the ducks and then search for Gordie and Neil in Stevens Bay where they had planned to hunt. But when I got to the island, I found their boat parked at the floating dock. What a joy it was to catch them taking naps! Having only one bufflehead for their morning's efforts they had returned to the island to eat their lunch. Each blamed the other for suggesting a nap.

After showing off my eight northern bluebills, I had no trouble convincing the fellows to return with me to our hot spot. There we found Steve with his limit, enjoying his lunch. The birds were still flying and long before sunset we were filled-out for the trip.

When the guided hunters saw us return with reinforcements, they picked up their decoys and headed west. We named the island where they hunted, "Guide Island", and our own little spot, "Bluebill Island". Although we have had successful hunts on scores of islands, this island is the only one our camp still calls "Bluebill".

There are so many great memories of bluebill hunting on Lake of the Woods, including annual hunts on the Minnesota side of the lake with my old boss, Senator Ed Thye (former Governor of Minnesota), with Ted Rowell, Sr., of Baudette as our host, but the story I want to share next involves three Staples teenagers.

There is a special joy that comes with watching young people on their first successful hunt. The three neophytes were brothers Chris and Chad — whose non-hunting father had asked me to "take them along sometime"—and their buddy, Kev. My frequent hunting partner, Jerry, and his son, Greg, had come up earlier and hunted the day we arrived. They had a good shoot and Jerry suggested a point within view of their blind where they could see flocks of bills crossing from time to time. We were there before daylight.

Even putting out decoys was an adventure for the boys and they kept me busy answering questions about why we placed them as we did. I answered with explanations such as:

"We set up with the wind to our backs because ducks like to land into the wind."

"We leave an open space between two bunches of decoys because that will bring the birds in closer. They like to land in open water rather than in the middle of the stool."

First bluebill hunt — Chad Longbella, Kevin Crocker, and Chris Longbella.

"We put a string of decoys out away from the main bunches because Jerry had said the flocks were passing out a ways from the point. A line of single decoys farther out will get their attention — hopefully."

As sometimes happens, the bills didn't fly that morning until about 9 o'clock. About the time the boys were sure the birds had all gone south while we slept, the first bundle of bills swung in from the right — they had come from the big water to the west and were headed for more sheltered feeding areas. If it had not been for the outlying decoys they would probably have passed out-of-range, but they turned nicely and swung over our decoys, but then continued east — untempted by our display.

"Why didn't we shoot?" Chad asked. I explained that I was hoping they would make another swing and give us a better shot as they came straight-in. Then, I added, "If that's going to be their pattern for the day, we're going to have some pretty tricky shooting. It would be a whole lot nicer to have them come straight into our decoys. That makes for much better shooting. When they come in low and slow with their wings cupped and their feet stretched out in front of them it just doesn't get any better than that."

As I finished speaking, five more bluebills followed the example of the first flock, hesitating only a moment as they passed over the outer decoys. "OK", I said, "Here's the plan. Everybody watch to the right — I'll watch left in case we get fooled. As soon as someone sees birds coming, say 'Mark!' But just stay down. When I say 'take 'em' — start shooting."

Another fifteen or twenty minutes and I knew my crew was wondering if the flight was over, but about that time, Kev's sharp eyes picked out a good-sized flock of a couple of dozen birds approaching and gave the warning. True to the pattern of the day, they swung in range, slowing just a little, and I gave the order to fire. Twelve shots later two cripples were left on the water and they almost got away while we were reloading our empty automatics.

I think the boys expected the whole flock to fall when we shot, so I assured them, "Two isn't bad for a start." In truth, we probably lucked out, but with that many birds in tight formation and that much shot in the air, something had to fall.

As my Lab ("Mandy" this time) retrieved the ducks, the teenagers passed the birds back and forth, clearly thrilled by their first trophies. Each, of course, claimed jokingly that both birds were the ones he had aimed at.

The next flock was smaller — less than a dozen birds — and I'm pretty sure I was responsible for the one duck that did fall. Not being particularly comfortable with so many hunters shooting together and wanting the boys to know for certain that any ducks that dropped were theirs, I advised them that I was moving to the left of the decoys and would shoot "clean up" at the birds they missed. I would still be close enough to command the dog on retrieves. That position was a new experience for me. Trying to pick-off birds that had just been shot at and had shifted into high-gear proved quite a challenge.

Enough years have passed since that memorable hunt so that details of how many flocks came and who shot what are a little blurred, but I can recall an awful lot of flocks and an awful lot of shooting and quite a few shouts of joy as the happy young hunters connected now and again. I do recall that there was a lull in the action about midday but that the flights resumed about 3 o'clock as the ducks returned to the big lake. Fortunately we had a good supply of shells and fortunately darkness comes early that time of the year, or we'd surely have been out of shells no matter how many we had! Nevertheless, we did return to camp that night with a very nice bunch of ducks (The camp logbook reads "21 bluebills"). The boys regaled the other hunters through and after dinner with a shot by shot and bird by bird account of the day until bedtime mercifully provided an escape. But this was, and remains, a very special day in their lives and in mine. Even though each has experienced greater successes since, we often speak fondly of their first hunt on the Lake of the Woods.

Having shared about the first duck hunt for Chad, Kev, and Chris, my memory fills with thoughts of other hunts since with each of them, because individually or collectively they have been my hunting and fishing partners so many times and they have also become my close and special friends. No longer teenagers, they have all married and have families, but among the more recent memories we share of successful bluebill hunts, I recall:

- leaving Chad on an island the first morning of a hunt while I returned to my truck, parked at the Morson Marina, to pick up my shotgun which I had forgotten the previous evening as we loaded the boat! When I came in view of the island where I had left Chad, it appeared he was under attack! Bluebills were milling everywhere around the island. Because of the distance, they looked like a giant swarm of mosquitoes. Just as I turned off the motor so as not to disturb them, I saw four ducks fall — and then heard the three shots — not bad shooting for so large a flock. We filled-out that day in record time. We still call the spot, "Record Island".
- the day Chris and I were guarding our decoys on another island. We'd been having excellent shooting. Suddenly there was a roar from behind us — a sound I can hear yet. Chris said later he thought it was an airplane approaching low from behind. I honestly thought it was a big boat. But it was an enormous flock of maybe a thousand bluebills! They came over and along both sides of the small island we were hunting on. In confusion and in awe we sat there for a minute or longer with ducks milling and landing all over the place. Big flocks have always been a problem for me, and when we finally did shoot, only three ducks stayed behind. I suspect Chris shot all three. Later that same day, we were all out of shells and one duck short of our limit. Chris went back to the boat and found one last shell under the floorboards. I was afraid he would miss, or, worse yet cripple a bird, but he came through with a clean kill and completed our limits.
- with Kev, there is a unique twist to the story. He was hunting with me and my nephew, Dirk, (from Nevada), and using my Citori

over-under. From the start that day the gun was not working properly. Kev had to move the barrel selector manually after each first shot. It was no big deal in itself, but it meant that as each flock of bills came in, Dirk and I would empty our guns — then there would be a pause — and then Kev would get off his last shot, usually at some bird nearly out of range. It was especially tough because Dirk and I would be standing there waiting and watching and sometimes giggling or making unhelpful comments. Luckily for Kev, more often than not the last shot did connect. Strange what we remember about a hunt!

### What I Have Learned About Bluebills

● Although, generally speaking, the more decoys the better, we have found that 25 or 30 magnum decoys work about as well as a large stool and are faster and easier to pick up.

● Bluebills can be dumb, and I have seen them come into decoys when hunters have been standing in the open on the shore or in a boat, but don't count on it. More often than not, staying well hidden will pay off.

● They like big water or at least being near big water. Small islands or points work best. However, if they are feeding in a bay, they will probably come back to decoys set up in that bay.

● Flocks of bluebills seem to follow the same flight pattern for each day; learn from the first few flocks.

● There are few easier shots than bluebills settling into your decoys, but a bluebill flying overhead or across your vision is a difficult target. If you are missing, the odds are you are not leading enough.

● It really isn't all that important to be in your blind at daybreak — unless you want to be sure you get some favorite spot. Sometimes bluebills will not fly that first hour or two and it will pay to see where they are working before you set up. On most bluebill hunts I have had to move at least once during the day. I could have saved that time and effort if I had waited for daybreak and until the birds began to move around.

● Just because you don't see ducks in one part of the lake doesn't mean there are no ducks. It pays, very much, to explore.

● Look for rafts of ducks and set up as near as you can in the direction they are working.

● We have rarely done well the second day in the same location. When there have been exceptions to this rule, I assume they have been birds that arrived overnight and have not been shot at.

# CHAPTER II
## WOODDUCKS

*The woodduck — excellent on the platter, but almost too beautiful to shoot!*

Nearly every fall, during the last week of September, a "northern flight" of woodducks shows up on the Lake of the Woods. The experts tell us that woodducks do not nest north of the Minnesota-Ontario boundary lakes, and, indeed, they may very well not nest very much farther north than this — but I do know that there are sometimes a good many more woodducks on the Lake of the Woods the end of September than on the traditional opening of September 15.

There are, of course, woodies around for the duck opener, because many do nest on the lake. In fact, residents of the Lake of the Woods have helped increase their numbers by putting up duckhouses. We have learned, by the way, that woodducks are more likely to use these houses if they are located well back in a rice bay. Houses placed on islands or facing open water are more apt to attract goldeneyes.

Over the years, most of the woodducks we have shot have shown up in our bags as odd ducks, taken along with a teal, pintail, or widgeon shot while hunting mallards. But there are many good memories of that last week in September when woodies have been the dominant bird taken. It was on one such late September weekend several years ago when my then teenage nephew, Bruce, and I headed north after school on a Friday afternoon with woodies on our minds.

Even after all these years, I still don't enjoy the 8 mile trip at night to my island — especially on a windy, rainy night when you can't see a rock or even an island until you almost run into it. But this night was different. There was a full moon and tall Norway and white pines were silhouetted on the horizon like friendly sentinels showing us the way. The light breeze caused enough ripples to make the moonbeams dance on the water. It was a quiet night, and when we reached the island and turned off the motor and began to unload, we could hear the loons talking to each other all over the lake — their calls echoing off the high, rocky cliffs of the Alneau Peninsula.

We lit a fire in the Franklin stove to take the chill out of the cabin and then made preparations for the hunt to save time in the morning. Our 14-foot Alumacraft hunting boat was turned "right-side-up" and a dozen mallard decoys placed in it where it would be easy to put our hands on them in the early morning darkness. Unlike bluebills, woodies tend to move at daybreak and dusk, so we planned to get an early start. Returning to the cabin, we laid out our hunting clothes and made sandwiches for the morrow's hunt.

It has been said that "anticipation is greater than realization". I don't know how often that is true, but I do know that anticipation has given me many a restless night before a hunt. That night was no exception and the five o'clock alarm came way too soon. Pancake breakfasts are traditional in our camp the first morning of a hunting or fishing expedition, but in our haste to get going they are seldom enjoyed as they should be. We don't record what we eat in our log book (but just about everything else), but I'm quite sure that particular morning we stayed with our tradition.

The moon had set by the time we started out for a favorite rice bed, towing our duck boat behind, in total darkness. We had to use our flashlights to locate the spot we had in mind for our decoys. After dropping Bruce and Sam (my Labrador) off on shore I paddled the boat to a hiding place where I still had to wait for daylight before cutting through the woods to the blind. When it was light enough to move through the tangled brush and trees, I started into the woods. About halfway, I was startled but delighted to hear my nephew empty his automatic. I stopped to listen and finally heard what I wanted to hear: his command to Sam, "Fetch!"

I stepped into the natural blind just as Sam presented the second of two woodies.

"Six came; two stayed," Bruce reported, "A drake and a hen."

I couldn't resist picking up the drake and almost fondled it as I admired the bright feather patterns and the bill that looked like it had been hand-painted.

A flurry of activity followed. Singles, doubles, and another flock of six came in the first hour — usually announced by the familiar woodduck whistle, causing Bruce to observe, "If they'd keep their mouths shut they probably wouldn't get shot."

"Maybe there's some wisdom in what you say for us humans!" was my reply. His remark was an appropriate observation, especially that morning, as almost all birds snuck in low or came in from behind us, just over the willows. If they hadn't whistled, we may not have seen them until it was too late.

By the end of that first hour, Sam had made a total of five trips and had retrieved seven birds: six woodducks and a teal. The dog, in his fifth year, had become quite a show-off by sometimes retrieving two birds at a time.

As the sun came up, it brought with it a gorgeous day — not a good duck day — but a great day to be on the Lake of the Woods. The aspen and birch were in their full golden color and a lone maple was in its crimson glory. The air was cooler than the water and a light fog began to rise all over the ricebed. It was a relatively poor rice crop that year, but it has been our experience that this means more productive hunting than a thick, heavy stand.

We had plenty of time to enjoy the beauty of the morning, because after the initial flurry, there wasn't a bird in sight, anywhere, for more than an hour. However, with seven birds in the bag and some good hunting behind us we were content to stay put awhile and see what might develop. It was worth the wait. About 9 o'clock a pair of mallards began circling our ricebed. A few flops of the Scotch duck call reassured them and they came in, wings set, just to the right of our decoys. It was all too easy and our shooting was unexplainably bad. Oh, we got them all right, but shells #7 and #8 were required to finish off a cripple. They were young birds. The greenhead was nearly in full color, however, except there was no sign yet of a curly-tail.

It was another hour and a thermos later before anything more happened. We had settled back and were visiting — the decoys out of our vision behind the natural blind of cattails and rushes in front of us — when we heard that unmistakable sound, twice: "plop .... shush". Two bluewing teal had come from who-knows-where and lit in our mallard decoys. I enjoy eating 'most any ducks but I especially enjoy bluewing teal — and neither escaped.

With only three birds to go for our daily limits, we decided to wait it out. Lunch time came and we were still short three ducks. But as so often happens, midday brought more activity, and the enjoyment of our sandwiches was pleasantly interrupted, first by a single greenhead that foolishly crossed over our decoys, and secondly, by a pair of woodducks that flew in from behind over our heads, whistled once, circled, and then came in with landing gears down. Our shooting practice that morning finally paid off and we each downed a bird with our first shots, clean kills.

It was a memorable day: beautiful scenery, cool but not cold temperatures, good conversation, an enjoyable lunch in the duckblind, and we were back at the cabin in time to do a little fishing — picking up a half dozen walleyes and a couple of respectable northerns.

The next morning we chose a different rice bed, for two reasons: first, because there had not been all that much action in the first spot, and, secondly, because as we have said before we have seldom done well in the same location two days in a row. We arrived at the new spot, just as there was enough light to see what we were doing. A mixed variety of more than a dozen ducks took off as we entered the ricebed — a good omen.

Woodducks again provided the early action and we bagged four — and with improved marksmanship. Next, two teal flew by and we dropped one. About mid-morning a single mallard came in, and stayed. Then nothing for a couple of hours. "Well, Bruce," I broke about fifteen minutes of silence, "We've got a nice bunch of ducks, what do you say we head back to the island, clean the birds, and get an early afternoon start for home?"

"Might as well," he responded, but with a little reluctance in his voice.

We both stood up, and as we did, we heard a whir of wings overhead as a dozen or more frightened mallards began clawing for altitude. With probably more luck than skill we scratched two out of the flock. They plummeted down in the willows behind us, giving Sam an easy challenge.

"Now I'm ready to go home!" Bruce announced, and headed for the boat.

We didn't quite fill out, but we learned long ago that limits are not required for a successful trip.

Bruce and I were also together on another successful woodduck shoot — memorable more because it was the only time this particular combination of time and place paid off for us than because of the number of ducks bagged.

The occasion was again late September and we had spent a most frustrating day looking for ducks. It was one of those years when the rice was so thick and the water was so shallow it was impossible to penetrate even with a canoe. There were ducks around, lots of them, but they came in high, circled, and then dropped into the middle of a rice bed — never coming within three gun-ranges. Everywhere we checked the experience was the same. In a full day of hunting, after putting out and picking up decoys three times, we had three mallards and a woodduck to show for our efforts — and were lucky to have them. Yet, we had seldom seen so many puddle ducks so early in the season. As we were heading home at sunset, Bruce pointed across a ricebed and said, "Hey! Look at that!"

Flock after flock of ducks were coming into the rice bed at its far end, just over the trees, and landing in the middle. "If we were under them we'd be in range," he observed.

"Yeah, but it's too late," I replied.

"Too late for tonight, but how about tomorrow night?"

I agreed, and so it was that after another almost duckless day (the log book says "two teal") we made the difficult walk around the rice bed to the spot where the ducks had come in the night before. Because of the lack of action that day, we were in position about two hours too early. There was almost no activity until the last half hour of shooting time. And then they started to come — from somewhere behind us — woodducks — lots of them. Small flocks, big flocks, singles, doubles — all woodies.

Pass shooting is never easy, but once you find the proper lead, it can be very productive.

Bruce found the proper lead.

I never did.

Sam, the Lab, nosed out a total of nine fat woodducks that fell that evening between the trees and the rice in fairly heavy grass. I think I could honestly claim only two of them. But all in all, it was a memorable and a very satisfying experience. We had finally out-smarted them.

Several times in the years since we have tried or have observed the same location, but have never had a repeat experience. Where all the woodies came from, we do not know, but the map shows a little creek about a mile back in the woods. Our theory has been that beaver may have created a little lake that year where the ducks spent their daytime hours, but we really don't know.

Just one more woodduck experience before closing this chapter. The players were friend Jerry and his brother Roger.

We had discovered an unusual concentration of woodducks back in a long, narrow ricebed, bordered by tall trees. It was too late in the day to chase them out and use decoys in the hope they would return, but

Jerry proposed a plan. "You guys post at the mouth of the rice bed. I'll go around through the woods and sneak on them. If I get some shooting, fine; if I don't, you guys should do all right."

"Sounds good," I said.

"Yeah," Roger agreed, "But I'm about out of shells."

"No problem," Jerry responded, and handed him a big handful of reloads.

Within the half-hour, Roger and I were posted and Jerry had made his sneak. Now, I forgot to add, there was another member in our party, my new dog, misnamed "Super Lab" by the kennel; I had shortened his name to a more appropriate "Soupy". The dog was big, enormously enthusiastic, and very strong. To make sure the young dog didn't spoil the shooting, I tied him to my belt and that was a mistake; I should have tied him to a tree.

Suddenly, the ducks began to come — all woodies — and Jerry began to shoot. They came by Roger and me in nice range, but we were twin disasters. Every time I shot, a split second before I pulled the trigger Soupy would lunge at the passing ducks! I doubt if any of my shots came within ten feet of a bird.

Roger was also having trouble. He emptied his gun three times and didn't drop a single duck.

Minutes later, Jerry showed up, saying, "I need the dog; I've got six lying back there. They just kept getting up back in the cattails and I had plenty of time to reload — twice. How did you guys do?"

"Terrible," we replied as one.

I told my story first, and an unsympathetic Jerry doubled with laughter. Roger told his story and then just kept saying in bewilderment, "I just don't understand it."

Hours later, Jerry confided to me (and days later to Roger), "I knew I had made a mistake on those reloads I gave Roger; they were short on powder. I've waited ever since season opened for someone to borrow shells!"

But that isn't quite the end of the story. I should have recalled this experience that next summer when on a family outing at my cabin on Lake Shamineau, Jerry suggested we shoot some trap. He had a box of clay pigeons along and just enough reloads he wanted to get rid of. (You are probably ahead of me by now.) Yes, Jerry inserted each shell as he passed his shotgun to each of several shooters. Each did respectfully well, except me — I missed all six of my opportunities. Hours later, I made a connection between the woodduck hunting experience and my poor trap shooting. When I made the accusation, Jerry replied, "Close — but your reloads weren't short on powder — they were loaded with rifled slugs!"

## What I Have Learned Over The Years About Woodducks
- Woodies are on the move in early morning and late evening.
- Wooducks will often feed back in very heavy cover — like thick cattails. When jump shooting, it is often helpful to make a good deal of noise before assuming there are no birds and leaving the bay. Beat on the side of the canoe or even yell.
- They love acorns. Look for wooducks near oak trees.
- Woodies are attracted to remote beaver ponds.

# CHAPTER III
## MALLARDS

The mallard is truly the King of the Ricebed. Not only is it majestic in size and flight, but few birds are as handsome as the greenhead in full color with its iridescent head feathers, chestnut breast, vivid blue wing spectrum, curly tail, and bright orange feet. And for most hunters, it is without equal on the dinner table—particularly with wild rice stuffing and giblet gravy. What a trophy!

There have been many memorable mallard hunts for me on the Lake of the Woods, but among the more cherished was several years ago when friend Ralph, (a Minnesotan transplanted in Colorado), his teenage son Dave, and outdoor partner Gene flew in to hunt ducks. Ralph has his own plane, making it possible to come for even a weekend hunt.

The three hunters flew into Baudette on a Friday evening. It was a dark, blustery night late in October. I waited for them inside the terminal building — fully expecting a call that the weather had forced them to turn back, but it was actually a few minutes ahead of their scheduled arrival when I heard their Bonanza make its first pass over the airport. After warm greetings all around we headed for the lake.

"What's the duck report?" Ralph wanted to know.

I replied that a trip by friends earlier in the week had been lean on bluebills but a few northern mallards were beginning to show up. I didn't tell the whole story — actually, they had been very nearly skunked! I just didn't have the heart to dampen my friends' enthusiasm.

After a quick stop across the border for licenses and other supplies, we drove on to the New Moon Landing resort where my boat was waiting. There we found we were up against a strong northeast wind — almost a gale — with low clouds and total darkness. As we headed for the island it began to rain, and that coupled with the almost freezing water the wind picked up of the wave crests made travel most uncomfortable.

"I think we'd better stop overnight at Neil's cabin," I suggested, "I don't like to even think about some of those open stretches that lie ahead."

"You're the guide," Ralph responded.

"Yeah, do what you think is best," was Gene's confirmation.

And so we picked our way in the darkness to our friend's cabin on Big Raspberry Island. I knew Neil wouldn't be there, but he had told me where he had hidden a key for just such an emergency. We went to sleep with the rain pelting the roof and windows.

The rain stopped sometime during the night but the strong wind continued. We decided to wait for daylight for safer travel. We had brought in enough groceries for breakfast so we enjoyed the traditional first morning meal of pancakes and venison sausage. By the time dishes were washed and put away there was enough daylight to head out. In the remaining six miles to the island, we never saw a single duck. "Not very encouraging," Ralph observed, "but I guess you warned us there weren't many birds around."

"Don't give up yet — this late in the season the flight has to show up 'most any day," was the best encouragement I could offer.

Our stop at the island was just long enough to unpack the Lund Tyee, tie the 14-foot Alumacraft behind, and throw in sacks of both mallard and bluebill decoys. We were prepared for any opportunity.

In the apparent absence of bluebills, I suggested we check ricebeds for mallards. The first half-dozen stops, however, resulted in our seeing only a bird or two with a maximum of one small flock of six or seven in a sheltered bay about two miles from the island. When friends come so far to hunt, one wants so badly for them to be successful that my spirits were dropping with each empty spot. What little hope I had left was based on the knowledge that mallards — if left alone — can congregate in large numbers in one location even though not found elsewhere. As we worked our way west towards the big water, I did see a couple of bundles of bluebills and was just thinking about setting up for bills when the next stop — a long, narrow ricebed, produced what I had hoped and prayed for. The rice was fairly thin that year and as I nosed the boat into the bay there were explosions of mallards getting up at a half-dozen or more locations — perhaps a hundred birds in all!

There was one concentration of birds in a sheltered area near the mouth and another in a pocket deep in the ricebed. We decided that Ralph and son Dave would setup in the deep pocket, and Gene and I would hunt near the open end. What followed is truly a good memory. The mallards began their return, in small bunches, almost immediately after the boats were hidden and we were positioned in our natural blinds.

Ralph and Dave drew first action as a half-dozen big, northern ducks made a quick circle and then swung into their decoys. After a volley of six shots, three birds were on the water. The sound of their guns had scarcely died away when a pair of mallards came straight for our decoys — so confident of their safety that they didn't even bother to circle to check things out. It was a picture book opportunity. We shot almost simultaneously and both birds folded. As the bright orange feet of the ducks marked the spots where they lay in the weeds, Gene observed, "That just made the whole trip worthwhile!"

His remarks were punctuated with a single shot deep in the ricebed. We had seen nothing but learned later that Dave had bagged a single greenhead that had slipped into the bay through the tree tops and plopped into their decoys. The next half-hour or so brought no new action, but it gave us time to enjoy the stark beauty of the leafless trees and contrasting rich green of the spruce and pine bordering the ricebed.

"There is no doubt winter is just around the corner," Gene observed, pointing for emphasis to the crystal fingers of ice nearly covering the little puddle of water on the inside of our cattail blind.

And then more ducks arrived — a sight we still talk about. There must have been a hundred mallards that came in from the open lake in a long string. Most passed over our decoys, some hesitating as though they were going to land, but all passed on into the ricebed — heading for Ralph and Dave. When they reached the pocket, they gained a little altitude and began milling and circling. Suddenly, a small part of the flock broke for our end of the ricebed and the rest followed. They again slowed as they approached our decoys, tipping their wings as if to land. One hen actually did touch down — but only for a moment. And then they were gone — all of them — and they did not come back.

"Why didn't we shoot?" Gene asked rhetorically; he knew the answer. Everybody was waiting for everybody else and neither pair of hunters wanted to spoil it for their friends.

"I just hope that flock wasn't the bunch we jumped out of here," I worried, "If it is, this could be a long day."

But as I spoke, the words died on my lips, because several birds appeared just then through the tree tops across the bay. And they kept coming — I suppose about a dozen in all. They swung directly towards our decoys, their orange landing gear sticking out in front of them. "Now," I whispered.

We emptied our guns and four fat mallards were left flapping in the weeds and rice.

With our attention on our own birds, we didn't see the slightly smaller flock that flew into the bay; we only saw those that escaped following the shots of our partners. We learned later that Ralph and Dave had added three more to our bag.

The next birds over our decoys were somewhat a rarity for late season on the Lake of the Woods — a small flock of pintails. I don't know if there was a difference in their approach from the way the mallards had come, or what, but after six shots only one bird was down; however, it was a beauty — a full-colored, long-necked drake.

Kev Crocker with some hefty mallards. The author did help some. (See grouse story).

You may have noticed, dear reader, the absence of any mention of a dog. At this point in my hunting history, old Sam was gone and my new Lab pup, "Soupy", just wasn't ready.

Because of our late start, by this time it was already past noon. In our eagerness to get hunting that morning, we had not taken time to pack a lunch, so I suggested, "I think I'll run back to the cabin and make some sandwiches and fresh coffee. But first I'll pick up our ducks and theirs and see if they have any cripples that need looking for."

"Sounds good," was Gene's reply.

As I picked up their birds, Ralph and Dave assured me that there were no "crips", so I advised them of my plans and headed in. I made a good supply of sandwiches and then threw an elk roast Ralph had brought with him into the oven for supper. Good eating goes along with good fellowship and experiencing the out-of-doors as the most important reasons I love to hunt and fish so much.

I returned to learn that the action had continued and the boys had filled out. What a pleasure it was to know that the trip was now also a success in terms of game bagged and we had the luxury of just sitting around enjoying good food, hot coffee, and beautiful scenery. A few more mallards came our way and we just watched them plop into the decoys at one end of the bay or the other.

"We've got a few more hours of daylight; what do you want to do?" I asked.

"I'd like to hunt partridges," Ralph replied, "We don't have them in Colorado and there's no bird more tasty."

Dave and Gene expressed their agreement, and we went in four different directions into the woods. Once a few rods in from the lake, the brush and trees thinned out and made for easier walking and, equally important, easier seeing. Occasionally a shot would be fired (I only saw one grouse, but scored) and when we returned to the boat at dusk we had six birds in all.

That night, over the elk roast, we reconstructed the day and talked about how getting game wasn't really all that important for having a successful trip, but we did have to admit that it would be nice having birds to bring home after traveling so far.

The next morning I knew better than to return to the same ricebed, but the pressure of success the day before over-powered experience and daybreak found us standing guard over the same two stools of decoys in the same exact locations. After all, I rationalized, we didn't see ducks anywhere else and some ducks had come in after we were through shooting and they had no reason not to return. By mid-morning we managed to pick up a few stragglers — all singles and doubles — adding a respectable six birds to our total — and all mallards.

After an hour or so without any action, Ralph and Dave joined us in our blind. "Dave has never shot a bluebill," Ralph said, "We saw a flock fly over and would like to give it a try in the couple of hours we have left."

"Sure, go ahead," I agreed.

"I thought we'd try Record Island; I have good memories of shoots out there and it's close by," he concluded.

Gene and I stood guard until one o'clock, the agreed quitting time that would give my guests time to fly home yet that day. We never saw a solitary duck. About noon we heard a single shot from the direction of Record Island. When the boys showed up, on schedule, Dave was holding high his trophy — a rather scraggly looking hen bill, but he couldn't have been prouder.

"Now I'm ready to go home," he said, "Shooting my first bluebill was my only goal for the trip!"

Many other mallard hunts come to mind, some successful, some not. But the more memorable trips have something unique about

Bluebills, ready for plucking.

Jerry Hayenga at work with the duck plucker.

them. There was the time, a couple of years ago, when Staples friend, Gordie, and I stumbled onto some mallards the last weekend in October. We really had bluebills on our minds because we had seen a couple of large rafts on our way out to the camp on Friday evening. Early the next morning, therefore, we headed for the area where we had seen one of the rafts of ducks and an island we had nicknamed "Brushy Tip" — because of the two brushy blinds we had built on each end of the island. It was a blustery day with frequent gusts of wind and occasional snow in the air. The birds seemed to be on the move almost every direction we looked. Filled with optimism, we set up our decoys in front of the leeward blind.

It was one of those trips when birds were landing in the decoys while we were still setting up. By mid-morning we had filled out and we devoted the rest of the day to fishing (poor results) and partridge hunting (the log book says seven birds).

The next morning we awoke to an entirely different weather system. The sky had cleared and the wind, which was light, had shifted to the west. We headed out pre-dawn and as we passed the mouth of a small ricebed we flushed out a large flock of birds. It was too dark to identify them but I guessed, "late migrating ringbills" because of where they were located. We set up on a rocky island near Bushy Tip but the bluebills seemed to have vanished. We sat for an hour staring at our motionless decoys and an empty sky. Getting bored, I told Gordie, "I'm going to take the boat and check out those birds we flushed this morning."

As I rounded the point protecting the ricebed, about 50 or 60 *mallards* rose into the air. It was then that I saw that the bay was frozen over and the mallards were feeding in the only rice standing in open water — at the mouth of the ricebed. I hurried back for Gordie but found that he had dropped two birds from a big flock of bills and wanted to stay there. He offered, however, "I'll drop you and Queenie (my new lab) off at the ricebed. I'll check on you in a couple of hours or so."

We had to go back to the island for some mallard decoys so quite a bit of time elapsed between the time I had jumped the ducks and when we set up. No ducks had come back. I was beginning to have some doubts. But no sooner were the decoys in place and Gordie out of sight than a unique return of the mallards began — one bird at a time. The first duck came in perfectly, quacking to announce her arrival, and I dumped it just short of the decoys. And that established the pattern. About every fifteen or twenty minutes a mallard would show up and decoy perfectly, coming through the tree tops across the bay and straight in, never circling. It wasn't long before Queenie and I had our six birds. Shortly thereafter Gordie showed up. He had two more bills but when he saw how well I was doing on mallards he said, "Move over, I'm coming in!"

I replied that it was time for lunch and volunteered to return to the island to prepare it. "Besides," I added, "I think even you can handle one duck at a time."

When I returned to Gordie and Queenie I found that he had another four ducks; each had kept faith with the pattern. I had brewed a pot of chili and made a few sandwiches so we settled down to lunch and conversation and waited for the two additional birds we needed for our limits (It was the last year we were allowed late season bonus bills). But nothing showed. We finished our chili. An hour passed, not a bird.

"Well, I guess that's it," I told Gordie, "We'd better pick up and clean our birds so we can start for home at a decent hour."

I started to stand when Gordie cautioned, "Mark!"

In came not one but five mallards; two stayed.

We never have figured out why nearly all of the mallards came one at a time, nor whether they were from the flock I had originally jumped — but I guess we really didn't care!

Another unique mallard hunting experience is also memorable because I shot one bird at a time — but not because that was the way they came. It was because my automatic had malfunctioned and reduced my gun to a single shot.

Chad Longbella and the author — the day his automatic became a single-shot.

My young friend, Chad, and I were hunting the same ricebed as in the previous story. We had flushed about 50 mallards as we swung into the bay and so we set-up where most of the birds had been feeding. It wasn't long before they began coming back. Chad had a ball; I had frustration.

Most of the birds ignored our decoys and settled in about a hundred yards to our right. So Chad moved down and I guarded the decoys. We had a great shoot but my contribution was meager as a result of my handicap. I did find, however, that I took a good deal more time on that first (and only) shot and that did make a difference. But when a dozen big northern mallards come into your decoys and you have only that one shot and then you have to watch the rest of the ducks, or sometimes all of them scramble for altitude while still in good range, that's hard to take! Yet, the memories are now good ones and this particular trip would not stand apart so clearly from all the others if my shotgun had worked perfectly.

## What I Have Learned Over The Years About Mallards

● Mallards are perhaps the most intelligent of ducks. Respect that intelligence.

● Use natural cover as a blind when possible. Keep hidden. Especially, keep your face down.

● In contrast to diving ducks, the hunter does not need a lot of decoys. I have never used more than a dozen and have had some excellent shooting in remote spots where I have carried in only two decoys because of long or difficult walking.

● Sometimes decoys aren't necessary. If you jump mallards in some bay where they have been feeding awhile, they will likely return to that spot even without decoys. Because they often circle before landing, it is likely you will have some good shooting. You can tell if birds have been using the spot for awhile by looking for feathers in the weeds or along the shore and droppings on the shore.

● Never try to chase down a crippled mallard in the water with your boat; it will dive and you will probably never see it again. They can swim with just their bills out of water or may dive and hang onto a weed with a death-grip. I have seen mallards do this in clear water where they can be easily seen. When prodded with a paddle they broke loose and came up dead.

● Rarely will there be good hunting in the same location two days in a row.

● Keep looking for mallards. Several times I've jumped only a few or no birds in bay after bay, and then found a hundred or so mallards in some secluded spot where they hadn't been disturbed.

# CHAPTER IV
## RING BILLS
## (Ringneck Ducks)

Ring bills have been described as bluebills that think they are mallards. And it is true that, although ring bills look very much like bluebills (scaup), they are found in quite different habitat, frequenting shallow bays and even ricebeds in contrast to the deeper waters which attract most diving ducks. Generally speaking, ring bills are more difficult to hunt than their big water cousins. Ring bills do not decoy readily; oftentimes the best shot is as they cross in front of the decoys. They rarely come straight in, eager to land as bluebills do. But there is something very special about the way they will drop into a secluded bay at hell-bent speed with the wind rushing through their wings, looking and sounding very much like miniature jet planes.

At the time of this first adventure, Curt and Jon were teenage neighbors living north of Staples. We had enjoyed an earlier hunt on the Lake of the Woods that fall (September), but it had not been real productive. This fact made me especially anxious to show the boys a good hunt. It was the first weekend in October and I figured our best chance would be ring bills or the first wave of northern mallards.

We arrived at my island early that Saturday afternoon and wasted no time unloading our food and duffel and throwing sacks of decoys into our boat. By 3 o'clock we were bay hopping looking for ducks — either mallards or ring bills — in numbers large enough to encourage setting up our decoys.

The first two bays we visited had produced ring bills in earlier years, but that day we kicked up only a few scattered ducks. On the third stop we hit pay dirt. It was a fairly large ricebed but with fairly thin vegetation and a few pockets with no rice at all. It had produced good shooting over the years for both ring bills and mallards. We pulled into the mouth of the bay and I cut the motor as I stood up to look around. At first, nothing flew up, but then well over 100 ring bills took off from a pocket back in the right-hand corner. It was an ideal spot because we could use the natural cattails and brush growing on shore as a blind.

We paddled the 16-foot aluminum boat I was using at that time for hunting back into the bay and set out three dozen regular size bill decoys. I have not had real good luck with magnums on ring bills. As I dropped the boys off on shore, I announced that I was going back to the cabin to throw a venison roast in the oven. We were expecting three friends from St. Cloud (Jerry, Harry, and Steve) to join us by supper time. As I pushed off I said, "I want to see nine ring bills belly-up in the decoys when I get back!"

I don't know where the number nine came from—it just popped into my head. But when I returned about an hour later, Curt stood up in the blind and yelled, "Count 'em!"

I complied and counted out loud. When I stopped on "eight", Jon pointed to a clump of cattails where another bird lay half-hidden. "You missed one," he said with a laugh.

"Did we follow orders or what?" Curt asked.

I had figured the boys would have some action, but nine birds was well beyond my expectations. I quickly picked up the birds and hid the boat up the shore. Before I reached the blind, another small flock swung nicely over the decoys and two more birds dropped. One was a cripple and in their excitement the boys blasted a decoy that got in the way. I have never repaired that decoy; it's more fun just keeping it around to tease the guys. The later it became the more the action, and we had our 18 birds by sundown.

Over supper the boys excitedly shared their experiences with the newcomers. After they finally wound down we made plans for the next day. Jerry, Harry, and Steve had been talking about Obobikon Lake crappies on their way up and decided to head there next morning. They planned to hunt early and then fish.

Jon and Curt were so anxious to return to the ricebed I agreed to give it a try but warned that it probably wouldn't be nearly as good as they had experienced. I suggested we start there but then work our way to Obobikon and meet our friends for lunch. The boys agreed, but a little reluctantly.

Next morning, as we reached the bay well before daylight, the whole corner of the ricebed where we had hunted exploded with birds. For about the first half-hour after daylight the action was fast and furious. Our gun barrels actually got hot! But when it was over it was over — not a bird in the sky from then on. We had done well, however, and were within four birds of our limits when the boys finally agreed to pick up well after mid-morning.

We checked out several bays on the way to Obobikon Lake but saw few ducks. We met our friends on schedule on the first island inside the channel (we call it "lunch island" because we often rendezvous there to eat). We shared chili and stories. Jon and Curt had by far the most to tell. Jerry, Harry, and Steve had found no concentrations of ducks anywhere, but had enjoyed some pretty fair crappie fishing — good enough so that I deserted Jon and Curt in a little bay where we jumped about a dozen ring bills and joined the others in fishing. I made the better choice because when I picked up the boys at sundown they had one bird to show for their efforts.

"You should have left us back where we hunted this morning," Jon chided.

"Yeah, we'd have filled us out," Curt added.

But both agreed on the way home that it had been a good day and a super trip.

When I think of ring bills, I think of Steve (St. Cloud). He has an uncanny knack for locating ring bills when all others fail. I recall one hunt in the same bay where Curt, Jon, and I had so much fun. Just Steve and I were up that trip. On the way to my island from New Moon Landing, where I keep my hunting boat, we checked several spots for birds and in one small, hidden bay we kicked out a couple of dozen ducks of mixed species. I suggested he leave me there if he wanted to explore. Steve agreed, tossed out some decoys,

Steve White and our ring bills in the rain.

and headed for the island where he stopped only long enough to get rid of our food and gear. He had agreed to return in a couple of hours to check on me.

There was action early, I dropped a ring bill out of a bunch of three that swung by and two mallards that decoyed nicely. When Steve returned on schedule and picked up my birds I was delighted to learn my mallards were "blacks", somewhat rare in these parts.

Steve reported that he had found a sizable flock of ring bills in the bay I described in the previous story. He had set out his decoys and dropped two. Having seen nothing since the first few minutes I decided to join him. He was set up across the bay from where Curt and Jon and I had our shoot. He was using a fallen pine tree for a blind — up a bank and about ten feet above the water.

Just as we were in place, it began to rain — hard. But this didn't stop the ring bills from flying. The first flock swung by well out beyond the decoys. I considered them out of range but Steve emptied his Browning and scratched one out of the flock.

"Pretty lucky!" I observed.

"Luck or not that's about the way they all have come — and they don't circle back," was his reply.

Two very wet hours and lots of shells later we had our limits. The most we dropped from any one flock was two, but to my surprise we had to chase down only a couple of cripples.

Somehow you don't mind the rain nearly as much when you have that kind of action.

It was another rainy, miserable day when Steve and I had a good shoot on ring bills up in one of the ricebeds in the north end of Burrough Bay. There wasn't a lot of rice but it was raining so hard the birds didn't seem to notice our 14-foot Alumacraft hidden in the thickest stand of rice we could find, and decoyed about as well as ring bills decoy.

I had Lady, my English setter, along that trip because I intended to do some partridge hunting. She wisely crawled under my knees as I sat in the bottom of the boat and didn't move, not even when we shot.

Action was fairly steady on the bills and we picked off a couple of high-flying mallards that came within range in the rain. One actually fell into the boat and hit with a loud "thud" — that was the only time Lady raised up to take a look.

We didn't fill out until late and by the time we picked up our decoys it was totally dark and still raining. We even got lost for awhile trying to find our way out of the bay through the rice and rushes. Our friends back at the island became worried and were just starting out to look for us as we rounded the last point on Hay Island on our way home.

Interesting how a limit of ducks, a warm cabin, good food, and friends can make such a miserable day a very special memory.

Nephew Dirk Manoukian with his first limit of bluebills.

Speaking of ring bills brings to mind a special trip with my nephew, Dirk (then a teenager), from Reno. It was a November blue bill hunt on Miles Bay. There were few hunters and lots of ducks. We set up our decoys in a bay better suited to ring bills but we had kicked up a flock of perhaps a thousand late-migrating bluebills.

The action was fast and furious that afternoon and it didn't take long before we were approaching our limit (16 in those days) — all nice fat bluebills and most of them greater scaup. With one duck left to go, I told Dirk, "It's getting late, I'm going to get the boat. You better get that last duck before I get back!"

Mandy, my Lab at the time, followed me (unfortunately for Dirk). As I stepped into the boat I heard Dirk shoot. I pushed out and started the motor. As I came around a little point of rushes I saw a show I'll never forget. There was a floating bog just to the right of the decoys and Dirk's duck, a cripple, had come down just outside of the bog, but out of range from shore. Now Dirk, being from Nevada, had never heard of floating bogs. He had seen them on the lake over the years as we fished together but it never occurred to him that cattails with willows and small trees growing amongst them would be anything but safe to walk on. It looked like part of the shoreline to him. Dirk is a two-time high school state heavyweight wrestling champion and nothing was going to keep him from finishing off his duck. He hit the bog at full stride and his momentum carried him just far enough out from the solid shore that when he broke through he went down to his armpits! Somehow he was still able to see the cripple through the vegetation and finished it off with a single shot. When I picked up the duck from the boat I discovered that it was a gorgeous, late-season ring bill drake in full color.

I don't know which Dirk will remember the longest: the successful hunt, falling through the bog, or the long, cold ride home. But to make sure he wouldn't forget the experience I had the ring bill mounted for him as a Christmas gift!

## Other Species

One of the special things about hunting on the Lake of the Woods is the variety of ducks. One never knows what kind of a mixed bag will be the result of any given trip. Over the years, in addition to the ducks I have written about, we've picked up pintails, widgeon, gadwalls, black ducks, green wing teal, shovelers, canvasbacks, red heads, buffle heads, golden eyes, harlequins, scoters, and one ruddy duck.

Geese are fairly rare in our part of the Lake of the Woods and I suppose we've averaged less than one bird a year. But that's fine with me; otherwise I wouldn't have an excuse to hunt Saskatchewan or Manitoba!

### What I Have Learned About Ring Bills

● Look for them in big, shallow bays — but without too much rice.

● Our best shots have been in the evening.

● Keep the decoys in closer than for bluebills; most shots will be as they swing by beyond the decoys.

● Many ring bills are hatched right on the Lake of the Woods. They do not breed in the far north so most of them will come down early, showing up in late September or early October. Because shallow bays will freeze first, most ring bills will leave earlier than bluebills.

● Sometimes they will join bluebills on the open water and even fly with them.

Jon Edin and Curt Jenkins, both of Staples, Minnesota, pose by a pile of ringbills.

# CHAPTER V
## RUFFED GROUSE

I have to be honest. When it comes to grouse I'm a meat hunter! I so dearly love to eat this bird I will resort to most any legal means to put it on the table. My most favorite recipe is to cut the grouse into bite-size chunks, dredge them in seasoned flour, brown them in a cast iron skillet, and then cover the meat with a can of cream of mushroom soup mixed with a can of water. I then usually add some fresh (or canned) mushrooms and let the whole thing simmer (covered) for about an hour. I serve this over fresh, hot, buttered biscuits. I honestly don't know of any meal I enjoy more — not even lutefisk!

Do you still need some additional excuses for my shooting partridges wherever I find them? OK —

1. The brush is usually so thick, especially before the leaves drop, that you can't see to shoot grouse in the air.
2. It is challenging enough to walk so slowly and quietly and look so keenly to just see a bird.
3. I can't hit them in the air anyway!

I try to take time each and every hunting or fall fishing trip to do some grouse hunting, so I have many, many memories associated with this tasty bird. Among my best memories are those associated with hunting with Lady, my English setter. Lady was nearly pure white with reddish brown ticking and facial markings — a beautiful creature. So high-spirited, so affectionate. Although I bought her for hunting pheasant, she had a remarkable talent for hunting grouse — almost every bird she encountered flew up into a tree! My theory is that her light color somehow induced that response in the birds. They seemed to be very

Lady — my secret weapon for grouse.

curious about her and would stay, mesmerized, wherever they lit, usually with eyes focused on her. My challenge was to figure out which tree the bird was sitting in and to locate the well-camouflaged, motionless target.

Most of my memories of hunting with Lady are associated with neighboring Hay Island. The interior of that island is so beautiful — away from the thick brush and other growth along the shoreline. There are groves of aspen, small swamps and meadows, logged off areas, natural openings, and bluffs which provide spectacular views of the lake. And there are giant trees of every species, including some of the largest birch I have ever seen. Just the scenery and wilderness experience, even without the grouse, is reward enough for the time and energy expended. But usually hunter and dog left the island with a handful of birds.

When hunting without a dog, I have found a relatively easy way to hunt grouse. I choose shorelines with walkable beaches. As I move slowly along the shore, I look as far back into the woods as I can. The grouse seem drawn to the water and I believe I see more birds than when I work the interior. During the most recent peak in grouse population I picked up a daily limit of five birds several times in about an hour of walking.

It was during the most recent peak in the grouse cycle that I experienced one of those days when I seemed to be in the wrong place at the right time all day long. Kev (Big Lake), and I were wandering around the lake looking for mallards[1] but we also planned to hunt partridge. Our first stop was an island where we could do both. There was a secluded ricebed between that island and the next island which was unapproachable by water because of the low lake level that fall. My nephew, Bruce, and his son, Jack, had found mallards there the previous weekend and Jack had shot his first greenhead and also shot a couple of grouse.

Kev said he would check out the ricebed but I opted to take a walk for partridges. Queenie, my most recent lab, stayed with me. I had been walking for about a half-hour without seeing a bird when I heard Kev empty his automatic, and then follow up with two more shots — which told me he at least had crippled something. I promptly changed direction and hunted my way to Kev, still no grouse.

Jack Lund with his first two grouse.

When I arrived at the ricebed, I found Kev was waiting for the dog. "Got four mallards down," he reported cheerfully. "There must have been 50 of them in here."

While Queenie retrieved the ducks, I returned to the boat for my hip boots and half-dozen mallard decoys. I was almost back to the ricebed when I heard another volley. Three mallards had returned, (or they could have been new ducks), and two stayed.

I put out the decoys and we sat back to see what might happen. After an hour of empty skies, Kev suggested, "I think I'll take a walk for grouse."

"Might as well," I replied, "but I sure didn't see any when I was roaming around."

You can guess what happened. One hour and five shots later, Kev returned with his limit of grouse. In the meantime, a lone greenhead came in drifting across the decoys about 10 feet off the water — I can see him yet — flying away after three shots! And that is how my day went.

I did have some better luck in the afternoon, however, and we returned to the island that night with nine big, northern mallards, nine fat grouse, and another good memory.

### What I Have Learned About Grouse

● Although mornings and evenings seem most productive, I have had very good hunting on sunny afternoons — along sun-warmed hillsides.

● Partridges like to feed in young aspen growth—such as is found in recently logged-over areas.

● It pays to walk very slowly and to stop often, for periods of two or three minutes. Hidden birds will become nervous and "cluck" or start to move.

● Use a .410-gauge shotgun. It is lighter to carry and will do the job just fine.

[1] See picture, page 79.

Kev Crocker and two fistfuls of grouse.

# CHAPTER VI
## BIG GAME

I would like to begin with a bear story.

Actually, we were on the lake hunting deer. My partners were Leo and Ray (Jerry's dad), from Lowry, and Jerry's brother, Bruce, from Staples. It was back at a time when rifle hunting was permitted on the Alneau Peninsula.

That particular afternoon we had beached our boat below a relatively high bluff on Turtle Lake and had each gone a different way looking for deer. Our plan was to "still hunt" but move every hour or so, hoping, if not seeing a deer ourselves, to push one into another hunter. Over the years, this technique has worked pretty well for us.

Although I had jumped a couple of deer that afternoon, I had not seen enough of either animal to take a shot. The same proved to be true for my partners. Late in the day, I decided to return to a piece of high ground near where we had left the boat. It was my intention to pick a spot with good visibility and stay there until the end of shooting time, hoping one of my partners on the way back to the boat might run something by me. It had been a warm, quiet day and the woods had been full of activity, but every time I thought I had heard a deer it turned out to be a squirrel or a partridge or, one time, a porcupine. After a long sit on the bluff and with darkness coming on, I gave up and headed for the boat. As I was about to start down the cliff I discovered I was in the wrong location and the boat was actually about a quarter-mile up the shore. Knowing I could make better time on the more open, rocky, high ground I stayed on the bluff and headed in the direction of the boat — walking very fast. As I passed within 50 yards of a large clump of bushes, I heard some rustling. Having heard small animal noises all day, I hurried on, but the noise behind me grew louder, so I walked back. I could see something moving in the bushes. In retrospect, I'm sure it was the bear swinging its head back and forth. Suddenly, the animal burst out of the bushes, running parallel to me along the edge of the cliff—it was a nice black bear. My first shot with the .30-06 rolled it over, but it was on its feet immediately and continued running. I took another shot as it disappeared over the edge of the cliff.

It was growing dark and I figured I had a wounded bear on my hands. It was headed in the direction of the beached boat and, assuming the other hunters had returned, I yelled, "Wounded bear heading your way!"

They told me later that although they had heard me they did not understand what I had said. They assumed I had a deer and wanted help.

It was getting dark rapidly, by this time, and the heavily wooded area on the east side of the cliff was particularly dark. I carefully made my way down the steep hillside, rifle ready and peering into the gloom for a dead or wounded animal. About two hundred yards further along, between me and the now visible lake, I saw what I thought was either a big, black chunk of log or my bear. It was my bear — dead!

The author with his first bear.

About then the boat pulled up to the shore and I signaled my whereabouts. It was our first bear (a boar), and there was plenty of excitement. By the time I had finished my story it was dark. Bruce took out his rope and proceeded to try to tie it around the bear's neck so we could drag it to the boat. Somehow in the darkness, his hand touched the soft pad of the bear's front paw and he jumped back, saying, "Tie your own darn bear!"

The next day as we stored our boat at Phil Hanson's camp, (now New Moon Landing), on our way home, Phil checked the bear's teeth and announced, "A four year old."

It proved to be the best eating bear we have ever shot.

I have some wonderful memories of deer hunting, but the best memory of all is of my first big buck. In fact, it is the largest buck I have ever shot or in all probability ever will shoot — 262 pounds when weighed at the locker plant three days later.

My partners were once again Ray and Leo; Jerry was due up the next day. It was late October. The first evening we picked up a nice doe on the Alneau — just before dark. I had also taken a couple of quick shots at two departing deer that had been with the one we shot. Although I didn't find any blood, there hadn't been enough time before dark to do a thorough search. And so the next day, because I wanted to look for blood, we decided to hunt the same general area.

It was a beautiful morning, but not a good day for deer hunting. There wasn't a whisper of wind and every step in the very dry leaves made a loud crunching sound. I was certain I would never get near enough to a deer to see it — let alone shoot it, so I decided to go directly to the place where I had missed the deer and made no effort to walk quietly. The spot I was headed for was on a plateau northeast of Kawakimik Lake.[1] As I was trudging up the side of that hill, making an embarrassing amount of noise, I heard what sounded like hunters driving deer a couple of miles away. They were howling and yipping like wolves, and although it may have been the real thing, I still think it was hunters. It was then that I heard another noise, heading my way. I froze. The noise grew louder and nearer. And then I saw it, this enormous buck running full speed, level to the ground — head down. It passed me at about 50 yards. I emptied my semi-automatic — five shots. The deer didn't flinch or slow its pace. And then it was out of sight. I listened to the diminishing noise and then heard a final crash in the distance.

Fearing I had missed it completely, I hurried over to where it had run by. I'm sure my heart must have skipped a beat when I saw blood — lots of blood. It was then that I saw that the deer had been running on a trail and I followed it — eyes to the ground — watching the blood signs. A couple of hundred yards later, I looked up, and there lay my deer. He had crashed over a windfall and was lying on the fallen tree, facing me. From where I stood I could easily count the 10 long tines on his rack, five on either side, and some additional brow points.

I remember yet what I did next, I let out a warwhoop and then yelled, "Ray, Leo, come and see what I've got!"

The author and Ray Hayenga enjoy a well-earned coffee break after dragging out the author's first trophy buck.

Happy hunter, Don Hester, with 262-pound Alneau Peninsula buck.

On that quiet morning they had no trouble hearing me and come they did. While waiting for them to show up, I checked over the deer to see where I had scored. To my surprise, I hit it all five shots, but only two of the shots were lethal; the other three had not been effective. Fortunately, none of the meat was damaged.

We were a good mile from the boat, but we made a harness of rope for the lead man and the other two pulled on a stout stick tied with a shorter rope to the base of the antlers. From time to time we changed positions and rested frequently. It's amazing what three men can move pulling in unison. We wore the fur off one hind quarter!

By noon we had returned to camp and hung the buck alongside the doe — where we knew Jerry couldn't help but see it as he approached the island that afternoon.

Following lunch, we continued the hunt, but, very honestly, I didn't work very hard. I returned to the bluff where I had been headed when I shot the buck. A thorough search convinced me I had missed the two deer I shot at the night before. For the rest of the day, I positioned myself on a comfortable spot on the hillside where I could see any deer that came in the vicinity and proceeded to enjoy the gorgeous, relatively warm afternoon. There wasn't a cloud in the sky, but I knew the weather was about to change because I was treated to a great spectacle of hundreds of ducks and geese migrating in from the north. I have no idea how many flocks of ducks I saw, but I recorded in the log book that I had counted 33 flocks of geese and swans. The snow geese and huge white swans were particularly beautiful outlined against the bright blue October sky. It was the kind of a day when you wouldn't mind living forever!

Of course there are many other memories of hunting deer on the Lake of the Woods. We will never forget the enormous doe Jerry shot. In fact, we almost didn't take the smaller doe with it because in comparison it appeared to be a fawn. It turned out the larger animal weighed 182 pounds (it must be a record of some kind), and the smaller doe was 128. And then there was the time Don (Cass Lake), shot a buck which, by remarkable coincidence, weighed the same as my biggest trophy, (262#), but it had a smaller rack. The two deer were shot 200 yards and seven years apart. One very well could have been the son of the other. But one of my most vivid memories is of a buck that got away. It has taken a few years, but that memory has finally become a good memory.

I was hunting on the mainland and was working my way back to the boat to meet my friends Don and Ed (Motley), to return to the island for lunch. It was about 11 o'clock and I decided to find a spot to sit for about a half-hour before walking down to the lake. I came across a place where two deep game trails intersected, so I sat down with my back against a big tree. After only a matter of minutes I heard a deer working slowly in my direction. It seemed to be feeding as it walked. Once in awhile I could hear a branch go "ker-whop!" against its hide or hear the antlers rattle against the underbrush.

I caught my first glimpse of patches of brown at about 50 yards, but I couldn't see enough to shoot. Besides, it seemed to be circling towards me. It continued to come, slowly but unseen, for several minutes. The adrenaline was really pumping! Suddenly it was right there in the brush in front of me, quartering in my direction. Its antlers seemed to be tangled in the bushes and it tossed its head from side to side as it moved slowly forward. I knew the deer was mine! I took point-blank aim and squeezed the trigger. Nothing happened — not even a click. The deer was making so much noise I was able to flip out the shell and drive in another one. Again I squeezed the trigger. This time I heard a faint click but the shell didn't fire. As I re-loaded a third time the deer either saw or heard me or both, it bolted and was gone forever!

When I examined the misfired shells I found one of them had a dent, but the pin hadn't hit it hard enough; the first wasn't even dented. When I checked the firing pin I saw the cause of the problem — rust! I had been hunting moose and caribou in Alaska earlier that fall. We had experienced some very wet weather. I had dried and lubricated the rifle but obviously hadn't done an adequate job. After getting to my feet I walked off the distance — 13 paces!

To this day I always try out my rifle before a hunting trip. Of course, never a problem.

Although deeply disappointed at the time, I now cherish the memory of having that majestic wild animal so close to me for so long. The experience and the memory have helped give me a more appropriate perspective of what hunting and fishing are all about. Sure I enjoy eating fish and game — very much. Sure I enjoy the feeling of success and exhilaration that comes with landing a nice walleye or making a tough shot on a bluebill, But, bottom line, the fish and the game are good excuses for enjoying a wilderness experience along with the special fellowship that comes with enjoying the out-of-doors with others.

That's what good memories are made of.

## What I Have Learned About Deer Hunting

● Watch the wind. Deer have an incredible sense of smell.

● Make as little noise as possible. Their ears are infinitely better than ours.

● While tree stands are effective in areas frequented by hunters who keep the deer moving, they seem less effective in the sparsely hunted Lake of the Woods area.

● "Still hunting" has been effective for us. That means sitting for an hour or so where you have a good view of a game trail or other appropriate habitat, and then moving, very slowly and quietly for 20 to 30 minutes or until you find another good spot to sit. It is helpful if other hunters are doing the same thing in a carefully defined area.

● If you just walk through the woods, no matter how carefully or quietly, you may see a lot of deer but will probably have few good shots.

● While fishing in late summer or fall, keep an eye open for deer along the shore or check sandy beaches for tracks. You will have a good deal more confidence if you *know* there are deer where you are hunting — and confidence makes a difference.

● Drives can be very productive. Points and islands are most easily worked, particularly if you have only a few drivers. It will pay to carefully study charts of the lake.

● Check the laws. At this writing there are some areas where only primitive weapons may be used. In other areas guides are required. Sometimes property ownership or staying at a resort is required.

[1]Rifle hunting on the Alneau was then legal.